# ALGOSPEAK

# ALGOSPEAK

How Social Media Is Transforming
the Future of Language

## Adam Aleksic

ALFRED A. KNOPF • NEW YORK • 2025

A BORZOI BOOK

FIRST HARDCOVER EDITION PUBLISHED BY ALFRED A. KNOPF 2025

Published by Alfred A. Knopf, a division of Penguin Random House LLC, 1745 Broadway, New York, NY 10019.

Knopf, Borzoi Books, and the colophon are registered trademarks of Penguin Random House LLC.

Library of Congress Cataloging-in-Publication Data
Names: Aleksic, Adam, author
Title: Algospeak : how social media is transforming the future of language / Adam Aleksic.
Description: New York : Alfred A. Knopf, 2025. | Includes index.
Identifiers: LCCN 2024051333 | ISBN 9780593804070 (hardcover) | ISBN 9780593804087 (ebook) | ISBN 9781524712907 (open market)
Subjects: LCSH: Language and the Internet | Internet users—Language | Youth—Language | Social media
Classification: LCC P120.I6 A54 2025 |
DDC 402.85/4678—dc23/eng/20250411
LC record available at https://lccn.loc.gov/2024051333

penguinrandomhouse.com | aaknopf.com

Printed in the United States of America
Published July 15, 2025
Reprinted One Time
Third Printing, July 2025

The authorized representative in the EU for product safety and compliance is Penguin Random House Ireland, Morrison Chambers, 32 Nassau Street, Dublin D02 YH68, Ireland, https://eu-contact.penguin.ie.

*To Kirkland*

# CONTENTS

# ALGOSPEAK

# INTRODUCTION

···········

## Why Your Kids Are Saying "Unalive"

Y OU'RE A DIE-HARD Nirvana fan, and it's the thirtieth anni-
versary of Kurt Cobain's suicide. You want to pay your
respects, and you heard Seattle's Museum of Pop Culture is putting on an exhibit to commemorate the lead singer. When you
get there, however, you're shocked by the first placard under the
display. It doesn't say that your favorite singer killed himself. It
doesn't say that he "committed suicide." Instead, it tells you that
"Kurt Cobain un-alived himself at 27." Huh.

It's understandable if you would've felt upset in this situation.
In fact, so many museum visitors were riled up about it that
curators were forced to replace the placard a few days after the
faux pas went viral. The term "unalive" seemed to trivialize the
topic of suicide, making light of a death still felt by many. Even
more jarringly, it represented the first notable offline use of a
word made for dodging internet censorship.

"Unalive" might have been surprising to casual museum-
goers, but by that point it was already quite normal to middle
school teachers. That's because, if you spend enough time around

seventh and eighth graders, you're virtually guaranteed to hear them use the word as a synonym for "kill" or "commit suicide."

It might be a bully in a hallway telling someone to "just unalive yourself." It might be an edgy teenager saying they'd rather unalive themselves than clean their room. Or it might even appear in more formal contexts, such as student essays on Hamlet's contemplation of unaliving himself or classroom discussions on the unaliving that happens in *Dr. Jekyll and Mr. Hyde*.

These aren't hypothetical situations. Each of those examples was indeed overheard by one of the more than seventeen hundred middle school parents and teachers that I surveyed while researching this book. It might sound ridiculous to older audiences, but "unalive" is very much alive. In fact, it's the future of the English language.

For a relatively recent word, "unalive" can be applied to an impressive range of scenarios. It can show up in informal speech, such as the bullying example, or formal speech, such as the Hamlet example. It can occur in ironic or meme contexts: One teacher overheard their student say, "Let's go unalive some sandwiches."

Most important, the main function of "unalive" appears to be euphemistic. Many adolescents use it when they're uncomfortable talking about the concepts of death and suicide, since "unalive" sounds like a less scary word. While this development has caused much hand-wringing among adults concerned about trivializing suicide, it could very well be positive for mental health education: One 2023 Associated Press article argued that "unalive" makes it easier for counselors and students to have "meaningful discussion" over difficult topics,[1] and many of the teachers I talked to echoed this idea.

In some cases, students are even learning the word "unalive" before the word "suicide." It's what their classmates are more comfortable saying, and since it gives kids a new way to express themselves, "unalive" will probably only continue to grow in popularity. It's already begun creeping into more formal, educational settings, such as the Hamlet essays or academic discussions on Dr. Jekyll unaliving himself, because students genuinely perceive it as a classroom-safe alternative to its heavier synonyms. In a side placard, the Museum of Pop Culture gave this rationale for using the word:

> "Unalive" has sparked constructive conversations, especially among young people, addressing issues such as depression, anxiety, and suicide.

In many ways, this is nothing new. We have been euphemizing death as long as we've had language. The verb "to decease," for example, comes from *decessus,* the Latin word for "departure," which was introduced as a more agreeable alternative to the existing word for death, *mors.* Similarly, the verb "to die" was originally an Old Norse euphemism for the Old English verb *sweltan,* which was, in turn, likely also a euphemism for the even older English word *diegan* (related to "die" but then forgotten long enough to be reintroduced in a new form).

Clearly, even the stoic Romans and fearless Vikings got as queasy about death as modern middle-schoolers. It's only because we've been constantly running linguistic circles around our mortality that we still use phrases like "passed away," "left this world," and "departed." In that regard, "unalive" is just another step in this ever-evolving process.

The crucial difference, however, between "unalive" and "decease"—and the reason it came across as so offensive—is the context in which "unalive" emerged. The word first appeared in its modern verb form in a 2013 episode of *Ultimate Spider-Man* and then circulated on a few meme sites without ever gaining much offline traction.[2] After that, it might have been relegated to the ever-expanding void of obscure internet history had it not been for the Chinese government.

Starting in 2019, China began enforcing its censorship policies such that social media companies would be held accountable for short-form video content generated by their users. One of those companies, ByteDance, had a popular app called Douyin that was subject to these regulations; to adhere to these new censorship policies, it began aggressively blocking any content critical of China, including discussion of topics such as the Hong Kong protests and the Xinjiang internment camps of the Uyghur people. This was all accomplished through a new "sensitive words" tool that drew on an extensive library of high-risk keywords to identify and remove any instances of those keywords being spoken or written or somehow appearing on-screen. The keywords tool was then combined with a string of other AI-driven processes to create a personalized stream of recommended content we collectively call the algorithm.[*]

This "algorithm" was then applied to Douyin's international counterpart, TikTok. The exact vocabulary lists were most likely tweaked for the new markets, although we can't know for sure, because everything about them is shrouded in corporate secrecy. There is substantial reason to believe that ByteDance has suppressed anti-Beijing sentiment on TikTok,[3] and that it has previously censored content related to LGBTQ+ themes and other sensitive topics such as politics, pornography, and self-harm.

An unfortunate result of this policy is that it became very difficult for online creators to have earnest conversations about topics that might incidentally register as violations of the TikTok community guidelines, such as suicide prevention. Knowing that their video might be removed for talking about their own

---

[*] I'll keep calling this collection of processes *the algorithm,* since that's how we talk about it colloquially, but remember that it's a little more complicated under the hood.

experiences, some influencers opted to use lesser-known alternative words. This is how "unalive" made its way from a *Spider-Man* meme to become a widespread synonym for "kill."

Popularized through a few viral videos in early 2021, "unalive" exploded in usage and became a widespread online term from 2022 onward.[4] Eventually, it made the leap from TikTok to other contexts, such as video game streaming, where apps like Twitch also restrict discussion of suicide. At a certain point, some people started saying it primarily out of habit, or because they saw other people saying it. That's how "unalive" was able to make a second leap, from online to offline usage.

The middle-schoolers obviously don't know this. They aren't saying "unalive" to avoid algorithmic censorship. They do so because they see other people using it, and it genuinely does serve a very useful euphemistic function. Many might not even be aware of its origins: A majority of the teachers I surveyed were sure that at least some of their students didn't know where "unalive" came from. They simply hear it from content creators, or from their peers who are more active on social media, and then start using it because it's a helpful, versatile word that can be applied in a variety of situations. This kind of positive feedback loop ensures that, with time, fewer and fewer people will know the story behind "unalive." Eventually, more institutions like the Seattle museum will pick up the word to keep up with the youth, until it eventually becomes so normalized that its etymology is completely forgotten.

Honestly, fair enough. You probably didn't know where the word "decease" came from, unless you studied Latin or are some kind of etymology nerd. But I think it's safe to say that "decease" didn't happen just because it was impossible to carve the word *mors* into an ancient Roman tablet. We're entering an entirely new era of etymology, driven by the invisible forces behind social media and its algorithms.

·········

Traditionally, this kind of evasive speech is called *algospeak*. Fittingly, the word seems to have been created on social media: The earliest references to the term for "algorithms shaping how you speak" are from scattered tweets and TikToks before Taylor Lorenz popularized the concept in a 2022 *Washington Post* article.

The word was sorely needed, because algospeak is everywhere. A 2022 TELUS International survey found that three-quarters of Americans have encountered some version of algospeak online, with 30 percent actively using coded language to circumvent content moderation. I would venture that the numbers are a lot higher, since many people unknowingly come across or reproduce these words in offline interactions. Especially now that we have millions of middle-schoolers using algospeak in their daily lives, we'll only see it continue to grow more relevant.

As a linguist, content creator, and human being, I've always had a very strange relationship with language on social media. It's my research interest, my livelihood, and my social life, and I perceive it to an almost problematic degree. I can't record a video without fixating on my own word choice, and I can't enjoy an Instagram Reel without also linguistically analyzing some aspect of it. I find myself constantly noticing how the format of social media affects my expressive decisions and observing where they've probably impacted those of other creators.

Well beyond censorship avoidance, I see everybody mold their speech around algorithms anytime language spreads on social media. The personalized recommendation structure of the TikTok "For You" page was a critical vehicle in helping "unalive" expand beyond the context of a niche *Spider-Man* reference. Since the platform used keywords to identify people passionate about mental health, it was able to bring those people together to form an online community—one that needed a way to spread resources and talk about their shared experiences without worrying about their posts being removed.

Once the mental health community repurposed "unalive" to suit their needs, the term slowly filtered into other communities on TikTok, since the boundaries of in-groups are much more porous on algorithmically based applications. As more people encountered the word and found it practical, the concept exponentially spread until it fully became a part of TikTok's culture. To be on the platform was to be familiar with its algospeak. Eventually, it spread to other social media, and then over to offline settings, or IRL.

"Unalive" also shows how the diffusion of words has become indistinguishable from the diffusion of memes. In its earliest days, the concept spread only through joke contexts until it found a place as a serious euphemism. Yet this is now how all concepts spread on social media: We find something compelling, we share it, and it goes viral. This usually happens in the form of memes, which the algorithm picks up on and helps to circulate. Social media platforms want to promote the most compelling content possible, so it makes sense that words will reach us through maximally compelling mediums like memes rather than something more serious. "Unalive" is far more likely to spread today than boring, traditional alternatives such as "passed away."

To me, the old definition of "algospeak" is far too limited in scope. Algorithms aren't just giving us euphemistic substitutions; they're playing a *defining role* in every aspect of modern etymology. They shape who gets exposed to certain words, how those words spread, and how popular the words eventually become. Language and memes and metadata are one and the same—all of it shaping our vocabulary and identities.

On some level, we can tell this is happening. The reactionary backlash to the Kurt Cobain "unalive" exhibit placard wasn't just about censorship. It demonstrated our wariness over our own algorithmic dependence, throwing it into sharp relief through an elevated museum setting that was supposed to be separate from all that. Other euphemisms would not have been nearly as controversial, but this was an *online word* being used *offline*. Clearly, that boundary has started getting blurred.

. . . . . . . .

About half a dozen times throughout human history, we've reached inflection points that fundamentally changed the nature of our communication. The shift to writing allowed language to evolve beyond the purely spoken medium, marking the division between prehistory and history. The printing press increased literacy rates and brought about the standardization of language. The internet itself marked another inflection point, broadening public information and allowing the written replication of informal speech.[*]

We're now at a new inflection point, characterized by personally recommended, short-form video content. All channels of communication—advertising, education, news, entertainment—are gravitating toward the medium by necessity, because that's what people have been conditioned to consume. If you want to go viral, you must make short-form video, and that means that you must mold your language to the constraints of short-form video platforms.

In many respects, the algospeak era gives us a new medium to retell very old stories. It's incredible that we're seeing time-honored patterns—like the continued ways to euphemize

[*] David Crystal and Gretchen McCulloch both covered this inflection point phenomenally in their books *Language and the Internet* and *Because Internet,* respectively.

death—play out in a novel context. It's still the same process, just happening in a new setting and happening much faster than ever before. While it might have historically taken words like "decease" hundreds of years to catch on, "unalive" did the same thing in just a decade, thanks to the new medium of TikTok and its subsequent copycats, like Instagram Reels and YouTube Shorts.

We're not just getting new words, either: The new structure of social media has given rise to entirely new accents, dialects, grammatical rules, and morphological processes. It's driven by community guidelines, but also by the nature of virality, the tricks influencers use to grab your attention, and the way your "recommended" feed is formatted.

Shockingly, for something with such an enormous impact on our day-to-day lives and language use, there's very little research or literature covering the algorithmic inflection point. Part of the problem is that it's so new. Researchers might find it hard to keep up with the fast pace of language change, especially if they're of an older generation. By the time these changes reach widespread use among younger demographics, adults are only barely starting to catch on. Even when they do, they might gripe about how today's youth are being corrupted, without regarding their words as serious linguistic developments. I believe it will be decades down the line, when words like "unalive" are completely normalized, that they'll ever be rigorously studied by traditional academia.

Another problem is the sheer volume of information to process. With more than seven billion internet users uploading over 400 million terabytes of media every day (the equivalent of 20,000 Libraries of Congress), we're generating an obscene amount of data for linguists to sift through. This can easily be overwhelming. No matter how much work we put in, we're never going to come close to capturing the infinitude of linguistic variation that's out there in plain sight. Even for the few hundred slang words that seem most culturally significant at this moment, it'll take decades for etymologists to fully catch up. Online user-generated repositories like Urban Dictionary, Know Your Meme, and Wiktionary are genuinely some of the most useful records we have of how language is evolving, but you never really know what you can trust.

Last, there's the transient nature of pop culture. It can be very hard to tell which meme is here to stay and which meme is a fad; this could discourage researchers from investing time into something that might not be relevant for long. As I write this in the fall of 2024, much of the slang I mention is already outdated. What seems current to me now might be passé by the time you read this book. If you reread this down the line, you'll notice the same thing. Some words will be gone, while new words will have emerged that you could never have predicted or imagined. And that's normal.

One thing is constant, however: this overarching pattern of algorithmic media causing linguistic innovation. Personalized recommendations aren't going anywhere for the foreseeable future, because the social media landscape is too competitive. Any country that has banned TikTok, for example, immediately saw rival apps like Instagram swoop in to dominate user attention. Short-form video is simply the most addictive medium we have, which means "the algorithm" is here to stay. This is why I think it's absolutely worth talking about even the most fleeting words. We must, if we want to understand where we're headed as a society.

"Unalive" is the tip of a colossal iceberg. Beneath the icy water, there is a hulking mass of creative techniques, trends, memes, identities, echo chambers, and new ways to commoditize language that only could have existed in the new algorithmic context. It's about time we started talking about it, so I invite you to join me in navigating our new linguistic landscape. Throughout this book, we'll dive into every corner of social media and together uncover the beautiful, chaotic idiosyncrasies of modern language. We'll find out who we are, who we're becoming, and what that means.

Great. Let's play Whac-A-Mole.

# 1

...........

# How to Play Linguistic Whac-A-Mole

REMEMBER WHAC-A-MOLE? The slightly unhinged arcade
game where new characters keep popping up no matter
how many times you smack them with your mallet? It might
seem ridiculous to use coin-operated violence as an analogy
for the serious linguistic changes we're experiencing online, but
Whac-A-Mole truly is the perfect metaphor for explaining how
humans react to censorship. As soon as a word is banned, we
find a way around it; that is, until content moderators catch wind
of the new word and ban that, too. Then another word pops up,
and the cycle repeats, trapping users and platforms in a never-
ending loop of new spellings and substitutions that disappear
once the algorithm catches on and the mallet comes down again.
The faster and better the moderation tools are, the more words
will be created. This is because the underlying idea—and our
desire to talk about it—remains.

People have been playing this game since the early days of
the internet. Frustrated with text filters on bulletin boards in the
1980s, netizens turned to "leetspeak," a hacker dialect charac-

terized by creatively respelled words. Since terms like "suicide" were censored in some chat rooms, leetspeakers wrote out coded replacements like "5U1C1D3" in much the same way that people began using "unalive." If the chat-room moderators caught on, they could just change the spelling to another easily recognizable form, like "$U!C!D€."

The tools being used have since grown more sophisticated, but the underlying process remains the same. Rudimentary word identification scripts might have been upgraded to fancy, AI-powered algorithms, but censorship is still driving linguistic creativity. If anything, the algorithmic era has spurred more innovation, because the game is happening faster, with more guesswork involved. Due to intellectual property concerns, not much is known about how these apps actually recommend content. Influencers are often subject to the whims of unknown and unfair criteria, with only opaque community guidelines as reference points.

This marks a major difference between leetspeak and algospeak: You could always immediately tell when leetspeak worked, because you would see your comment successfully posted onto a message board. For algospeak, however, the goal is to make it onto a user's "recommended page," and it's much harder to tell when you've successfully done that. Videos with sensitive keywords aren't always removed outright. Sometimes, they'll be "suppressed," or shown to fewer followers. Creators can also be "shadowbanned" without warning or notification. We—and I'm including myself here—receive very little communication from the platforms, so we're not sure whether videos do poorly because they're bad or because they're being censored. Understandably, then, we'll err on the side of caution when it comes to euphemization.

Creators *can* sort of tell what does and doesn't get onto the recommended page by looking at our video analytics. If I usually get most of my views from the recommended page, and then all of a sudden a video is getting views only from the "followers" feed, that's a semi-reliable indication that some part of my video made the algorithm unhappy. Through this kind of trial and error, influencers can extrapolate a pretty good idea of what the algorithm rewards and penalizes, and it's in this context that "unalive" was forged. When the word "suicide" wasn't getting views, people turned to the next best term to tell their story.

While linguistic innovation like this is an exciting and normal thing, it's reasonable to be alarmed at the way community guidelines are shaping important conversations, especially as people increasingly turn to short-form video for news or advice. Oftentimes, the mysterious rules governing social media are arbitrary or outright discriminatory. TikTok has historically been proven,[1] for example, to artificially suppress videos by "ugly," old, and poor creators, because they're not as appealing to new users. This means that it's often difficult to include larger audiences in discussions about things like disability, age, and income inequality. Nevertheless, we have no choice but to play the game and tiptoe around community guidelines wherever we can.

........

In 2022, the Charles Dickens Museum began a desperate social media campaign to get itself un-shadowbanned from TikTok. Whenever users would search for the museum's account, nothing would show up. Instead, they would be cautioned[2] that "this phrase may be associated with behavior or content that violates our guidelines" and that "promoting a safe and positive experience is TikTok's top priority."

Of course, the Charles Dickens Museum wasn't doing anything wrong. They were mostly posting house tours or excerpts of old letters. Instead, the problem was with the TikTok algorithm, which was flagging the museum's videos as obscene because they included the keyword "dick." For all its fancy high-tech machine learning, the algorithm had fallen victim to a classic internet pitfall: the Scunthorpe problem, named for an English village where residents discovered they were unable to create AOL accounts because their hometown contained the word "cunt."

Following an intense #FreeDickens campaign on Twitter, TikTok eventually agreed to unblock Charles Dickens–related search terms. However, it still remains difficult to curse—intentionally or accidentally—on any platform. While your videos won't get removed outright, they'll often be suppressed in search just like the museum's. Especially if you're cursing too much or too severely, your content will be hampered by the algorithm. If a video is eligible for the recommended page but still contains mature language, TikTok and Instagram will prevent it from appearing in clusters of similar videos in a user's feed, which means that it'll be pushed to a smaller audience than its work-safe competitors.[3]

Likewise, on YouTube, creators posting videos with severe or repeated profanity have to contend with "demonetization," where they lose the ability to earn revenue from advertisements on their content. This is especially scary to influencers whose livelihoods depend on a steady income stream from their videos.

All this means that we have a lot of reasons to respell our swear words creatively online. If you look up the keyword "bitch" through TikTok's search function, for example, you'll likely encounter variations such as "btch," "b!tch," and "b*tch" in the video captions. Same with "fuck," which will probably give you "fck," "fvck," and "f*ck"—none too different from the leetspeak letter substitutions of the past.

The practice of respelling offensive words is a centuries-old tradition known as *bowdlerization,* named for the Englishman

Thomas Bowdler, who is mainly remembered for publishing some egregiously family-safe edits of William Shakespeare's plays.

Self-bowdlerizing to avoid media constraints is not new: People have been doing it since at least the days of early newspaper comics, where sequences of graphic characters called *grawlixes* are still used instead of swear words to circumvent stringent syndication standards. The earliest known example is from this 1901 *Lady Bountiful* comic by Gene Carr:

Over time, some grawlixes got less thinly veiled as cultural norms against profanity loosened up. Cartoonists began drawing on symbols with a visual similarity to the letters they were replacing: "@##" and "$#*!" are now industry standards for the words "ass" and "shit." Fast-forward to today, and influencers are re-creating this process in social media captions. Words like "fvck," "b!tch," and "@ss" are born out of the same motivations, drawing on the same cultural tradition of bowdlerization.

Until the twentieth century, the preferred method of bowdlerization across all media formats was the double em dash
(——), typically replacing the entirety of a word save for a few
identifiable letters. Grawlixes marked a turning point, and the
asterisk (*) became more widespread for its ease and simplicity.
Around this time, symbolic swearing also shifted to replace individual letters, specifically vowels. The primary reason for this is
intelligibility: There are simply fewer options to go through when
guessing the meaning of "f*ck" than with "*uck," which could
also mean something like "suck." It's the same reason the vowel
is omitted in truncations like "fck" and "btch" on social media.

Another option is to change the word to something similar,
but funnier. If you're trying to sneak past robotic censors, why
not make it a little silly? You can easily swap letters to spell words
like "fukc" and "bicht," or drop them entirely to make "fuk" and
"bich." You can also up the goofiness by replacing consonants
entirely, like with "fucc" for "fuck" or "ahh" for "ass."* One can
also add humor or shock value by "swearifying" relatively innocent words, like "m*n" for "men" in some feminist circles of social
media, or "Tr*mp" for "Trump" in political circles. However we
choose to bowdlerize, there are so many profanity options that
we don't have to stop at evading content moderation filters—we
can also parody that reality.

········

Back when I was just getting started on TikTok, one of the
first videos I made was on how the words "pen" and "pencil"
are entirely unrelated.** In the video, I described how "pencil"
actually traces to the Latin word *penis,* meaning "tail"—and, yes,

---

* Both of these examples are taken from African American English; we'll discuss how
that happens in chapter 7.
** Still one of my all-time favorite etymology facts.

that's also the source of the English word "penis." Being uninitiated to the platform, I included the full word in my captions and received a content warning that TikTok wouldn't let me post the video. I went back and edited the spelling to *pen\*s,* which worked, although the video still performed much worse than other videos I was posting around that time. I realized that my video was probably being suppressed by the algorithm and felt very frustrated that I was restricted from making certain kinds of educational content.

Because I wanted my content to be seen, I begrudgingly refrained from discussing any other sexual etymologies. This, however, isn't an option for the many creators on social media making educational content on health, medicine, or sex positivity—which should have been permissible according to the TikTok community guidelines, but was still suppressed. It's easier for the algorithm to categorically penalize a word than to distinguish between use-specific exceptions.

As a result, even trained medical professionals on social media will regularly replace the word "penis" with "p3nis," "pen1s," and the eggplant emoji, 🍆. If they want their content to be seen, these creators have to get inventive with captions.

Well beyond doctors and sex educators, emojis are by far the most common way to substitute pornographic words on social media. It's very common for any creator talking about sex to use 🍆 instead of "penis" in their captions, and 🍑 instead of "ass" or "vagina," to a point where I've seen people physically say "eggplant" and "peach" when describing genitalia online. Along with 🍒 for "boobs," these substitutions all draw on visual similarity to the things they refer to, which I think is rather poetic. Written language emerged from the increasing abstraction of pictographs, and now we're looping back around.[*]

---

[*] While writing this book, I decided to test the algorithm by posting a video about the semiotic implications of these emojis. It was very well put together, but unsurprisingly

The entire field of semiotics is dedicated to studying "signs" like these. In the same way that public facilities use 📞 for "phone" and 🚻 for "restroom," the eggplant, peach, and cherries are symbolic substitutions for a concept. Emojis are just repopularizing that kind of communication through a new medium.

Many risqué creators have also used 🌶, literally interpreted as "spicy" or "spicy time" but figuratively understood to mean "sexy" or "sex." While these terms were already around before social media, they've definitely been popularized by short-form video: Google Trends shows searches for "spicy time" escalating in recent years, and I've been noticing more and more friends saying "spicy" since TikTok popularized the phrase.

Most of our sexual emojis are notably based on some kind of food product, drawing on a long-standing link between food and sexuality. Fruits, especially, have a history of symbolizing sensuality in art, while their names often function as colloquial terms of endearment, so it's not surprising that we would revert to more evocative emojis for pornographic algospeak.

Outside sexual food emojis, there are a few other algospeak symbols drawing on shared meanings (think 💩 for "shit"), but many others instead rely on acoustic similarity. The ninja emoji (🥷) stands in for the n-word, the corn emoji (🌽) works as a replacement for "porn," and the grape emoji (🍇) is understood as a common stand-in for "rape." These substitutions depend not on physical resemblance but on rhymes or slant rhymes.

I've seen a lot of criticism of these emojis online, but this is exactly what Cockney rhyming slang was doing in the early nineteenth century. The expression "blow a raspberry," for example, came from "raspberry tart" being a common slang stand-in for the word "fart," in the same way that "corn" now replaces "porn."

received a hundred times fewer views than my usual videos, with very few of those views coming from the For You page.

Once again, we see people drawing on age-old processes to sneak past online censorship.

········

Emojis are just one of many ways that people self-bowdlerize naughty terms. You'll still come across sex educators spelling the word "sex" as "s*x" or "s3x," but the most frequently used alternative in the early 2020s didn't involve a creative substitution or respelling. Instead, it introduced an entirely new sound sequence by modifying the *k* sound to a *g* sound.

I'm talking, of course, about the word "seggs," wholeheartedly embraced by creators in the infancy of TikTok. The hashtag #seggs has been used in more than 100,000 posts, #seggseducation shows up in more than 40,000 informative videos, and I've also heard my friends ironically use "seggs" offline.

Rather than just respelling the word to something immediately phonetic like "secks," people chose to make the word sound a little sillier, which is a very common pattern on social media. There's also "nip nops" for "nipples"; "peen" for "penis"; and "kermit sewerslide" for "commit suicide." These terms are all examples of *diminutives*—words meant to sound smaller, cuter, or less intense. It's the same reason a little kid might refer to his penis as a "weenie," "pee-pee," or "willy." Diminutives make words sound friendlier, and many people may be more comfortable using them online for that reason. Plus, sex is funny. These terms are all slightly goofier than their more serious counterparts, making them catchier and therefore more likely to go viral.

Many of these examples of sexual algospeak fall into the category of *minced oaths,* euphemisms created by slightly altering the spelling or pronunciation of offensive words. We've been mincing our oaths forever: That's why we say "heck" instead of "hell" or "gosh" instead of "God." Much like "peen," these words sound like a less intense version of what they represent, making them more palatable to easily offended audiences. We still understand what the words mean, but they lack the shock value to really upset societal sensibilities.

Minced oaths can also involve replacing entire phrases. In late 2021, the chant "Let's Go Brandon" served as a MAGA minced oath for the words "Fuck Joe Biden." Is that really so different from using "kermit sewerslide" instead of "commit suicide"? Both allude to more serious phrases through phonetic similarity, both became popular through their PG silliness, and both spread beyond meme status: I recently caught my Harvard linguistics friend ironically saying "sewerslide" in real life, which is exactly how these words start to enter the mainstream lexicon.

Upon finishing his 1948 book, *The Naked and the Dead,* the American novelist Norman Mailer was famously told by his publishers that he used the word "fuck" too many times for the book to be published. In response, Norman went through and replaced every "fuck" with the minced oath "fug," and the publication process went forward. I love explaining "seggs" through this anecdote, because creators using it instead of "sex" are doing exactly the same thing. By switching out a *k* sound for a *g* sound, they can skirt media censorship, even if we all still fully understand what they really mean.

. . . . . . . .

The more sensitive a topic is, the more it will be censored, and the more we'll find ways to talk about it. Multiple euphemisms for the same concept can fit slightly different contexts, making it harder for an algorithm to pick up on. If someone wants to talk about a sexual assault but doesn't want the frivolous connotations of the grape emoji, they can instead use the abbreviation "SA."

Initialisms like this have also been used to avoid censorship for thousands of years. Early Christians, for example, used a secret symbol called the Jesus fish to indicate their religion, since the Greek spelling of "fish" doubled as an acronym alluding to Christ. The Jesus fish was used as a signal between Christians to indicate to each other that they were in the same group, without being discovered by their Roman persecutors. Although the stakes for secrecy are not as high, "SA" is similarly employed by the survivor community to create a safe space for talking about experiences and sharing resources.

I recently came across another video in my recommended feed where a female college student posted about getting "red zoned" in her first week of college. This refers to the Red Zone of sexual assault, a statistical window between August and November when 50 percent of all sexual assaults happen at American universities. This sort of indirect speech is an example of *metonymy*, or referring to an idea through another, closely associated idea. The textbook example of this is referring to the executive branch of the United States as the "White House." When the student chose to describe her assault through the "red zone" metonym, she phrased her euphemism such that it would both be seen on TikTok and avoid triggering other assault survivors.

This type of evasive language has been getting more common, especially in political discourse. Rather than direct algospeak translations or euphemisms, many creators may skirt a topic while heavily implying its existence. In one 2023 video, a TikToker referred to Hitler as "the top guy of the Germans" because he was afraid of uttering his actual name on the platform.

The social media researcher Emily van der Nagel calls this "Voldemorting," since people are deliberately avoiding keywords in the same way wizards avoid saying the name "Voldemort" in *Harry Potter*. Van der Nagel first identified the concept in an era when people were using discreet language to prevent their content from showing up in searches for that keyword, which remains a very valid reason for skirting a specific topic. Almost every young person has at some point engaged in "subtweeting," the act of talking about someone online without directly mentioning them. Tricking search engine optimization tools like this can be especially helpful for creators who want to prevent trolls from finding and harassing them, and have plausible deniability if confronted.[4]

Much like Voldemort himself, though, the practice of Voldemorting has taken on a new life. It's now more about algorithmic optimization than search engine optimization, but creators can also use it humorously. Many influencers choose to refer to Donald Trump with words like "cheeto," "45," and "orange man," even if search results are unimportant to them and it's unclear whether social media apps actually suppress politicians' names. In effect, they choose to treat "Trump" as a *taboo word*—a term restricted due to a social purpose.

Taboos exist across a variety of cultures to avoid offensive practices like naming the dead or discussing menstruation, and creators are intentionally using that as a form of political and expressive power. By imposing a taboo on "Trump," or inserting an asterisk in the middle of "men," playing into algospeak puts the linguistic narrative back into the hands of the oppressed. The act of Voldemorting can indicate a lack of respect for the subject; it can also make a statement by reclaiming the act of censorship. By not talking about Trump directly, people signal that his name is filthy, too offensive to be uttered. Language, then, becomes an act of resistance.

. . . . . . . . .

Following the outbreak of the Israel–Gaza war in October 2023, social media users around the globe began voicing concerns that their posts about the conflict were being restricted on social media. TikTok and YouTube videos about Palestine were getting fewer views or outright getting removed, and the Pulitzer Prize–winning journalist Azmat Khan reported that her Instagram account had been shadowbanned for posting a story about the war.

Usually, platforms ignore addressing these kinds of concerns, or justify them through very vague policies. TikTok, for example, has rules nebulously prohibiting "highly controversial topics" and promotion of "violent or hateful actors," which it uses to suppress or remove content that can even adjacently be interpreted to praise Hamas. Because this process is automatic and relies on detection of specific keywords, many innocent videos ended up also being affected.[5]

I experienced this firsthand when I posted a video analyzing the phrase "from the river to the sea." The video was about how it is linguistically curious that two different groups can interpret a meaning so differently; I was just trying to educate my viewers and didn't take any stance on the conflict.

Of course, that didn't matter to TikTok's algorithm, which I suspect shadowbanned me for three days. My video flopped, with very little of my traffic coming from the For You page, and the new video I posted the next day got ten times fewer views on TikTok than when I cross-posted on Instagram. As someone relying on TikTok as an income source, I was terrified of losing my platform, and didn't know which phrases I could and couldn't say, so I stopped making content addressing the situation altogether.

But just as sex educators on social media had to find workarounds with words like "seggs," people making educational content about ongoing conflicts are forced to improvise. The month the war started, algospeak "translation tools" popped up online to swap out words like "Gaza" with content-safe replacements like "ğaza." Terms like "IDF" got replaced with substitutions like "IOF" (a derogatory shortening of "Israel Offensive Forces"). People began metonymically using the flag emojis 🇮🇱 and 🇵🇸 instead of writing out full country names.

Once the algorithm caught onto the 🇵🇸 emoji being used in "highly controversial" contexts, the game of Whac-A-Mole naturally continued. People began replacing the flag with the watermelon emoji, 🍉, in reference to its historical representation of Palestine during the Six-Day War. Due to its similar colors to the Palestinian flag, the emoji became a widespread symbol of solidarity and defiance.

Starting primarily with the 2020 Black Lives Matter protests, creators talking about race have similarly been abstracting their language online. It can be risky to say the words "Black" or "white," since TikTok has a policy suppressing or removing videos "exaggerating the ethnic conflict between black and white." Instead, influencers find loopholes like spelling "white" as "yt" and using the 🤍 emoji. Others take it a step further, simply using the palm of their hand to indicate the color white. This insertion of sign language isn't all too different from an emoji; both are symbols standing in for a concept.

In many of these cases, the creator is knowingly critiquing the algorithm at the same time as they acquiesce to it. Many pro-Palestine creators will start out their videos with an unrelated topic or a pro-Israel sentence before baiting and switching into their views on the conflict. This is intended as a wink to the audience, reminding them that the platform is always listening. In a way, the same is true for all of traditional algospeak: Even the eggplant emoji doubles as a metalinguistic reminder that your content had to pass through a layer of algorithmic perception.

. . . . . . . .

Every work-around goes out the window when we get to hate speech and slurs. All social media platforms are extremely clear on not allowing hate speech, and they enforce that guideline more deliberately than any of their other rules. Like other guidelines, however, these fail to capture nuance; as ridiculous as it sounds, there is a time and place for slurs.

For example, I once posted a video on how the word "fascist" is etymologically related to the "f-slur for gay people," which is the way I phrased it out loud. On-screen, I included the bowdlerization "f*ggot." Like my "river to the sea" video, it was entirely presented educationally, did not seem to offend anyone in the comments, and did not violate any rules.

Nevertheless, the algorithm must've caught on, since the next day I received a notification that my video was removed for a "Community Guidelines violation" and that my account would be suspended upon two more violations.

Evidently, self-censoring hate speech for pedagogical purposes can still be out-of-bounds for short-form video apps. How, then, is someone supposed to fully discuss the history of a marginalized community or the challenges they face? In many cases, the community guidelines designed to prevent hate speech end up impacting the very group they're supposed to protect. Consider the n-word, which the Black community should be entitled to use without repercussion. Instead, they risk removals and bans, meaning they must get clever with avoidant speech or ninja emojis.

In an unfortunate catch-22, this problem happens because minority groups' identities are considered "politically sensitive issues" by the algorithm. The keywords used by Black creators may overlap with the keywords used to talk about racism, because racism is frequently directed against the Black creators. But since discussion of racism is suppressed in the algorithm, many Black creators are inadvertently silenced. The same problem happens with homophobia and the queer community, or ableism and the disabled community. Now these groups can't even talk about the very problems that content moderation is trying to protect them from.

To make matters worse, actual bigots will use this knowledge to their advantage. Rather than making hateful content that'll get immediately removed, they'll often opt to mass-report videos of creators they dislike. Since reports on videos with "politically charged language" tell the algorithm to remove those videos, trolls find that they can effectively harass creators through this method.

Many creators are already afraid to use their community's vocabulary because of the perception that the algorithm is working against them. TikTok in particular lost a lot of trust due to occasional "glitches" like the #BlackLivesMatter hashtag showing up with zero views[6] or the exposés showing how it prevented undesirable creators from showing up on the For You page. Reading between the lines, these creators choose to find algospeak replacements instead of using their own language.

This is an incredibly relevant concern in the LGBTQ+ space. Beyond mass-reporting trolls and built-in bias politicizing queer identity, the community has to contend with direct geographic suppression. TikTok has openly admitted to censoring hashtags like #gay and #trans in conservative regions like Russia and the Middle East,[7] so, again, there's been ample reason to be suspicious of the platform. Murky or incomplete feedback only worsens the issue. Several American trans creators have complained about being banned without explanation—contributing to the justifiable paranoia even if their incidents had valid but uncited rationale.

As a result, many queer creators feel they must resort to algospeak to best express their identity. You'll see people use the word "zesty" or the 🪶 emoji as a metonym for "gay." In other instances, they've replaced the term "LGBTQ+" with phrases like "leg booty" or "alphabet mafia." The most famous example in the early 2020s was probably "le$bian" for "lesbian." While this might seem like a typical grawlix substitution, TikTok's text-to-speech function clearly didn't understand that, and would instead read the phrase aloud as "le dollar bean." This pronunciation was so wholly embraced by the online lesbian community that many creators started saying it out loud themselves.

"Le$bian" was always a joke for the chronically online. Kids in schools were never going to start unintentionally pronouncing the dollar sign, but it *was* a bellwether poking fun at how the algorithm is shaping our speech. Since its peak in 2021, the term has gradually been replaced by other substitutions like "wlw" for "women loving women," but I see these new terms as ironically *better* examples of algospeak, because people really are saying these terms offline.

The shift from "le$bian" to "wlw," the shift from "suicide" to "unalive," and all these other instances of linguistic Whac-A-Molery exemplify the *euphemism treadmill,* a concept introduced by Steven Pinker to describe the continuous motion of evasive words in the English language. The euphemism treadmill is why we're constantly updating our words for offensive things. The words "idiot," "imbecile," and "moron" all used to be serious words for classifying mental disability, but then they became negative, so we replaced them with the word "retarded," which also became negative, so we replaced that with "mentally disabled," which is also becoming negative.

The same process happens with terms for racial and sexual minorities as the words they use to describe themselves become poisoned over time. That's why "colored" became "black," and why some people now prefer capital-B "Black." Once words are used maliciously, we replace them until the cycle continues, as if moving along on a treadmill. This is a normal and inevitable linguistic process that can only really be solved by addressing the underlying societal problems causing the treadmill to move in the first place.

When the algorithm prevents people from saying "sex" or "suicide" or any other sensitive word, it becomes a proxy for human behavior. Instead of people turning a word negative over time, the platform labels it as undesirable for social media, causing the treadmill to move faster rather than actually preventing discussion of forbidden topics.

. . . . . . . .

Our colorful potpourri of euphemisms, bowdlerizations, and circular language is more than a collection of individual strategies to defeat content moderation tools. It's an entirely new style of communication serving a distinct social purpose.

What we're actually doing on social media is building up a common vocabulary to reflect our shared experiences. Human language is all about finding the best way to express our reality for others to understand us, and the "best way" constantly differs based on factors like social setting, communicative medium, and audience. In some academic or formal contexts, for example, the word "sex" is better expressed as "intercourse." On early TikTok, the best way to express the concept of sex was through the word "seggs." This wasn't just because it was algorithmically favored, but because of the cultural context in which it appeared.

"Seggs" became an indication that you understood the social expectations and dynamic of the online community. By opting to say it instead of a perfectly fine but lesser-used alternative like "secks," creators accepted the role the word played in shaping past online conversations and expected it to be a recognizable term for their audience.

This explains why words like "unalive" and "seggs" survived

well after it became clear that the terms were also being filtered by the algorithm. The terms took on a function of familiarity in the social media space, becoming shared terms serving an important purpose.

When considered together, these words constitute a *sociolect*, a form of language used by a particular social group. Sociolects are everywhere. The casual way you speak to your friends is a sociolect. The unique style of communication you use at home is a sociolect. The words you use online are the *algospeak sociolect*. In this mini-language, the "social group" encompasses all other people using social media.

American frat bros have a great example of a sociolect. When you observe them in groups, they speak the same coded language. Their voices will typically drop to a lower register and take on glottal fry. They'll talk about bringing brewskis to darties. Just like Instagram influencers, frat bros use shared terms of communication to better express ideas to each other and signal that they've accepted certain shared cultural norms.

When a frat bro addresses another frat bro in frat-speak, the communication is seamless, because it fits the social context. But imagine if Chad told Brad he was bringing "alcoholic malt beverages to the day party." Chad's meaning would still be communicated, but less effectively than if he used the words "brewski" and "darty." It would be weird for Brad because it's not in their shared sociolect.

At the same time, Chad would be much less likely to use the word "brewski" around his grandmother. This is classic *code-switching*—shifting between sociolects depending on the environment. Just as it's weird for Chad to suddenly lapse into stilted formal English when talking to Brad, it would be weird for TikTok sex educators to actually say "seggs" in real life. The context matters.

Linguists separate these sorts of situations into *domains of use*. Chad's frat house is a very different domain of use from Chad's grandmother's house, and he uses this information to speak differently in those environments. In the same vein, most people think of algospeak as exclusive to the online domain, so they won't say words like "seggs" in real life, unless the domains of use begin to break down or they're too young to fully distinguish them.

We get domains of use because of a psychological phenomenon called *communication accommodation*. Essentially, we're constantly making adjustments in our language (accommodating our communication) to be more or less like the person with whom we're interacting, because we innately try to attune to the behavior of others. Through this trial-and-error process, we determine what is and isn't appropriate in certain domains of use.

I think it's great for the English language that we're able to switch in and out of the algospeak sociolect. It's not some apocalyptic, these-kids-are-ruining-how-we-talk scenario, but rather an extra way of expressing ourselves that we've developed to fit a specific environment with specific constraints. We have the power to both use and not use it, and can seamlessly slip in and out of it to best articulate our thoughts depending on the domain.

One might expect this sociolect to internally differ between apps, due to slight differences in content moderation. However, algospeak on TikTok, Instagram, YouTube Shorts, and every similar platform is nearly identical. Successful creators rarely generate content for just one app, but instead cross-post to all of them, and as such try to work within the most severe algorithmic constraints (historically those on TikTok). Users, culture, and expectations will also often overlap across apps. Successful creators are usually in tune with that and make content that aligns with all at once.

Other commenters have previously pinned down the idea of an internet sociolect—the British linguist David Crystal identifies our exclusively online jargon as "netspeak"—but algorithms have now created an entirely new sociolect of their own. This goes well beyond the mere euphemisms we've previously associated with "algospeak," and instead characterizes the totality of how we understand each other on social media. As we'll start exploring in the next chapter, all "internet slang" words are brought to you by the algorithm, and all define the culture of being online. Whether it's "unalive" or a meme word like "skibidi," each linguistic innovation counts as "algospeak," and each constitutes a part of our collective identity.

········

Looking back at leetspeak—the earliest online sociolect, indicating belongingness to an elite group of internet-savvy users—a lot of its patterns are strikingly similar to algospeak. The word "porn" was often stylized "pr0n," to the point where it was eventually pronounced "prawn." Modern social media users are switching letter placements in the same way when they spell out words like "fukc" and "bicth," and also arrived at a food word with their euphemism "corn."

Both in the past and today, we progressively add layers of abstraction. Just as "white" became "yt" and "yt" became the gesture of holding one's palm up, leetspeak had levels of coded speech. The phrase "Alex is a boy" could be written in basic leet as "413x !z 4 b0j," but that could be taken up a level with the "extreme leetspeak" translation "413>< !2 4 |30`/." At a certain point, it's barely recognizable, but then again someone new to TikTok might be equally confused by a creator just holding their palm up to the camera.

Although leetspeak preceded emojis by more than a decade,

that didn't preclude early experimentation with pictographs. Message board users relied heavily on computer text art created out of common characters, like "8==D" for "penis." How different is that really from an eggplant emoji? Both are representations depending on a visual similarity, each a beautiful testament to humanity's commitment to finding new ways to depict male genitalia.

Leetspeak, too, was more than censorship: It was a *culture*, defined by its environment. There's no text-filtering reason to spell out "413x !z 4 b0j," but sentences like that were shaped through the zeitgeist of the early internet era, nuanced by the unique circumstances in which the sociolect was forged.

Is leetspeak any indication of the future of algospeak? It's definitely an imperfect comparison, because leetspeak had its own dynamic and was used by a much smaller group. The very reason it died out was that more people simply got on the internet, overwhelming the leet population and making h4x0rz behavior appear "cringe." Algospeak, meanwhile, is around in a time when *everyone* is on the internet and using these words, not just a select few. If anything, it's set to be around much longer and have a much wider impact than leetspeak.

Nevertheless, leetspeak had a pretty big legacy, considering its relatively small population of users. In many ways, it was at the forefront of a lot of linguistic internet trends, like "the" being spelled as "teh" in lolspeak. It also gave us actual mainstream terms, like "pwned" for "owned" and "noob" for "newbie." If that's any indication of where things are going, we'll probably see far more algospeak words reach offline usage, not least because of the breadth and speed of algorithmic language change.

Outside both leetspeak and algospeak, I'm again reminded of Cockney rhyming slang, created by petty criminals in London's East End to avoid detection by the police, but going beyond that to define a culture of its own. Whenever our speech comes under scrutiny, we respond by inventing sneaky solutions that in turn shape our identity. Language is, and will remain, one of the most important forms of power and belongingness.

When it comes to Whac-A-Mole, algospeak is just the latest iteration of a human constant. Like its historical equivalents, it has a certain domain of use, undergoes code-switching, and uses modified language to evade notice by the authorities. Our new video medium both influences and reflects innate cultural patterns, including—as you'll read in the next chapter—how those ideas spread.

## 2

..........

## Sticking Out Your Gyat for the Rizzler

IT SEEMS AS THOUGH everything happens faster on the internet. Each week brings a dizzying parade of new memes, fads, and slang words that evaporate as quickly as they materialize. It can be hard to keep up with the latest references unless you're spending hours a day catching up on social media trends.

Of course, it wasn't always like this: Look at Middle English six hundred years ago. Language was far more insular. Each city and region had its own, different dialect, to a point where there can scarcely be any discussion of a uniform "English" language as we understand it today. The only reason to adopt a new word was that it helped you better communicate with your fellow townspeople, so of course change came about more slowly.

Then England centralized, and the dialects of London and the East Midlands became the basis of what we now think of as Standard English. It was as if a switch had flipped: The upper class suddenly had a set vocabulary they could point to as "correct," meaning that all other dialects became "incorrect." By the

1750s, the word "slang" emerged as a catchall term to describe the nonstandard words used by the lower classes.

Around that same time, England became more connected than ever, meaning that more communities could coalesce to come up with slang. The lower classes especially felt freer to create new words since they weren't bound by the same rules, and wider social networks helped those words spread more quickly. If the upper class eventually started using those same words too, they stopped being called slang and became everyday language.

This acceleration was directly aided by the rise of print media. For example, in the mid-nineteenth century, there was an American slang fad to give words incorrect abbreviations, like "O.K." for "all correct." That was then printed in a Boston newspaper, helping it reach mainstream usage, which is how we have the word "okay" today.

However, newspapers had their limitations. They were—and still are—written in Standard English, which means they operate under the rigidity of upper-class linguistic norms. The later advent of radio and television media allowed more people to hear unfiltered communication, although even those mediums came with unique sets of content expectations.

Enter the World Wide Web, where anybody could post content for anybody else to see. Mankind finally became released from centuries under the reign of the language police, and new words sprang up from all the new corners of the internet. As early as the 1980s, internet users started making up slang like "lol" and "noob."

But this early internet era was the digital equivalent of medieval England: It was decentralized and disconnected in a way that didn't see much language change beyond the broad need to invent shared vocabulary. As the internet subsequently coalesced around large social media platforms such as Facebook, Twitter, and YouTube, our social networks (and thus our avenues for language change) expanded like a newly industrialized Great Britain, preparing us for the next great linguistic shift: the rise of short-form video.

. . . . . . . .

As a middle school student in the mid-2010s, it felt like every cultural reference could be traced back to Vine. During its short-lived but influential existence, the platform allowed users to post up to six-second clips, usually replicating a dance move or funny catchphrase. The videos dominated our collective consciousness in a way that only my generational cohort can truly understand. You couldn't walk down a school hallway without seeing someone dab, whip, or hit the nae-nae—all dances popularized by the site.

With these videos also came a slew of new slang words, like "on fleek," meaning "perfect," or "yeet," an interjection said while throwing something at high velocity. It also popularized existing words from African American English, such as "bae" and "fam," both terms of endearment for one's close friends.

These words were able to spread in the way they did because of the emergence of viral "trends"—popular internet fads characterized by rapid recombinations of some source material. The earliest trends replicated dances, but later iterations also spread as meme formats. "Yeet," for example, became widespread through a series of videos of a boy named Lil Meatball doing a dance, but humorously edited so that his friends would say "yeet" as he scored a basketball three-pointer or shot someone. The more edits that popped up, the more the term spread, until it began spawning its own trending formats, like another widely replicated video of a woman throwing a soda can while yelling, "This bitch empty! Yeet!" From there, "yeet" became an established piece of Gen Z slang.

This new dominance of rapid social media "trends" was uniquely enabled by Vine's short-form video style, since its content encouraged repetition unlike any previous medium. Although the platform was shut down in 2017 due to monetization issues, it had clearly tapped into something unique, and other companies were paying attention.

As Vine began dying out, another app named Musical.ly was emerging as its obvious successor. Like Vine, it relied on trend-based short-form videos, although the structure was more flexible (up to a minute), more focused on lip-syncing, and primarily filmed vertically (a response to the rise of smartphones). By 2017, it had reached 200 million users and caught the attention of ByteDance, which wanted to replicate the success of its own Chinese video app, Douyin.

Musical.ly was acquired and merged into TikTok, which is where ByteDance perfected the recipe by engineering the most addictive social media website imaginable. As soon as you opened the app, a rectangle of video would command the entire screen, while flashy colors and exciting content would make you completely forget about the existence of an outside world. Easily accessible in-app editing made it possible for anyone to hop onto the latest trend, go viral, and become a celebrity. Gone were the barriers to stardom posed by previous, long-form apps like YouTube. Now anything could and did happen overnight, while the only way to stay in touch was to constantly use the app.

But TikTok's main strength lay beyond its already impressive user interface. The platform's most important characteristic was undoubtedly its algorithm, which did far more than censor words. Powerful machine learning tools additionally analyzed every move you made: They tracked what you liked, what you commented on, how long you watched a video, and which profiles you viewed. All this got synthesized into your ever-changing feed, which predicted your preferences without you ever having to think about it. Don't worry, TikTok knew.

The algorithm was, of course, designed to maximize the amount of time you spend on the app, and it's worked: The average global social media user now spends more time on TikTok than anywhere else, which has left the other companies scrambling to catch up. In August 2020, Meta launched Instagram Reels, a similarly algorithm-driven vertical-video feature, and Alphabet followed suit with YouTube Shorts just a month later. It's clear that this style of content is the best way to hook viewers, and will be the dominant style of social media as long as we remain reliant on our smartphones.

The massive success of the personalized recommendation algorithm relies on a few tricks, but the underlying principle is quite intuitive: If you like a certain kind of content, you'll probably like other content similar to it. For instance, I recently liked a video of a man singing "Barbie World" by Nicki Minaj to the grave of President Lyndon B. Johnson. The algorithm correctly inferred that I enjoyed the song and sent me more funny "Barbie World" videos, which improved my experience on the app. It also probably pushed those videos to people who fit the same demographic profile as me, since they're also likely to respond positively.

When these songs accompany a meme or dance that people want to re-create, a trend is born. At its core, this process is the same as those on Vine and Musical.ly, just spread through a more sophisticated recommendation system. The videos are now especially compelling because they make it seem as if *everyone* were hopping onto a trend (a perception exacerbated by your biased recommendation feed). Because we're social creatures, your recommendation page will pressure you to watch or participate in these trends, so you can feel caught up on the latest cultural references. This turns into a positive feedback loop that has irrevocably changed the music industry: Numerous songs, from Doja Cat's "Say So" to Lil Nas X's "Old Town Road," reached *Billboard* No. 1 status primarily by becoming TikTok dance trends.

Songs like this were particularly important in the early days of TikTok, when it was still a music app and people wanted to consume videos of people dancing to songs they liked. Since then, of course, the app branched out to also play the roles of educator, journalist, and comedian, but the underlying strategies remained the same. If you're an entertainer trying to make someone laugh, you might set your video to a trending audio of a funny catchphrase.

In January 2023, for example, TikTok was inundated with the same sound bite of a woman saying, "Side-eye. SIDE-EYE." People around the world flocked to film themselves looking suspiciously to the side, captioned with a humorous explanation. The audio clip went viral in the same way that "Old Town Road" became popular: It turned into a trend that people were excited to replicate.

A few weeks later, a second, similar audio also went viral, of the phrase "bombastic side-eye. Criminal, offensive side-eye." Drawing on the popularity of the initial meme, but fresh with a newer, funnier catchphrase, the clip went viral in much the same way as "This bitch empty! Yeet!" rode on the coattails of the first "yeet" video.

It's easy to write off "side-eye" as yet another meme, but TikTok isn't some isolated, inconsequential vacuum. In the wake of the "side-eye" videos, Google Trends showed searches for the word spike tenfold and then consistently remain at a much higher search interest than before. People offline were saying the phrase far more frequently than they were in 2022, all because it was popularized online.

While the underlying linguistic process is quite similar to what happened with "yeet" in 2014, the rise of "side-eye" was amplified by TikTok's algorithm to have a much larger impact than it might have had a decade prior. Vine's video recommendation process was simple: It showed everyone the same popular videos, with the expectation that most people would like them. TikTok changed the game through its highly personalized recommendations. Rather than pushing just any video to your For You page, it cleverly learned to send you videos that should individually resonate for you.

Once the algorithm became aware that I enjoy both educational content and Nicki Minaj, for example, it sent me a video of the Depths of Wikipedia creator explaining how undersea fiber-optic cables work to the beat of Nicki's song "Super Freaky Girl," which is exactly the kind of content I want to see on my recommended page.

As soon as I reacted positively to the video, I got more videos about fiber-optic cables, because TikTok picked up on the fact that I'm interested in learning about them and sent me more videos with that metadata. (I really did enjoy the additional videos.)

The information felt special to me because I now had a personal connection to it, and this is how most people encounter viral memes nowadays. Audios like "side-eye" are introduced to your recommendation page through whatever unique iteration works the best for your specific profile, making you connect with it more than you might've on a more general platform. While I can count on ten fingers the relevant words from Vine, TikTok churns out new terms like "side-eye" every few weeks because everybody's seeing different things. Words have the ability to evolve coterminously without being overshadowed by a single popular "yeet"-style video that dominates everyone's recommended feed.

· · · · · · · ·

Creators are very familiar with how social media platforms recommend content, and we actively use this knowledge to our advantage. We very intentionally incorporate trending audios into our videos, because we're aware that the algorithm is more likely to push them to people who've previously shown interest in other videos containing that audio. As we've seen with "side-eye," this can mean that we unintentionally spread slang words at warp speed. My favorite example of this phenomenon is the "Rizzler song," a TikTok audio that went massively viral in late 2023 for its slang-heavy lyrics:

> *Sticking out your gyat for the rizzler*
> *You're so skibidi*
> *You're so fanum tax*
> *I just wanna be your sigma*
> *Freaking come here*
> *Give me your ohio*

While this may seem like gobbledygook to the uninitiated, each slang word referenced in the Rizzler song was already trending at the time for being associated with Gen Alpha comedy. "Gyat" is a synonym for "butt"; a "Rizzler" is an individual skilled in rizz, or seduction; and a "sigma" is a successful male. The words "skibidi," "fanum," and "ohio" mostly serve as nonsense words coming from other popular memes at the time.

When recombined into this song, the slang words formed an annoyingly catchy anthem heralding the emergence of a distinctly Gen Alpha style of humor. The internet was obsessed: Older generations were morbidly curious about this harbinger of their obsolescence, while Gen Z took to saying the words ironically or in intentionally "cringe" contexts. Posting even mildly interesting videos with the Rizzler audio was virtually guaranteed to get a lot of views, because so many people had shown interest in the song. As a result, videos using the song proliferated.

Just as social media now pushes trending songs or audios, it also pushes trending metadata, like words, captions, and hashtags. After all, the same people who were categorized as liking Rizzler-related content would probably also be interested in other videos containing the words "skibidi" or "gyat." The algorithm knows this. It looks at everything that might hint at your preferred content, and words are no exception.

Again, creators are very tuned in to this. That's why we use trending words, or even make certain videos in the first place. We know they'll do better if we talk about specific topics. In the wake of the Rizzler song, for example, we saw an explosion in remixes, covers, and explanations of it, from emotional piano remakes to a tutorial for how to sing the song as a liturgical-style Gregorian chant.* The creators of these videos made them because they *knew* the metadata would make them go viral.

I myself capitalized on this trend by making content explaining the etymology of the Rizzler lyrics. I racked up a million TikTok views for a video talking about the etymology of "rizz"; 2.5 million for "sigma"; 3.5 million for "skibidi." Yes, the topics personally interested me, but there are so many other topics that also interest me. I chose to focus on these particular words because I wanted my videos to perform better. Clearly, it worked, and I know I'm not alone in this: A 2023 University of Oxford study found that essentially all influencers are "purposefully

---

* The "Barbie World" singer mentioned earlier also ended up performing "Sticking Out Your Gyat for the Rizzler" at the final resting place of Lyndon B. Johnson.

minimizing their own creativity in order to pander to perceived algorithmic tastes and subsequently enhance their visibility." This affects not only our choice of content but also our aesthetics, creative processes, and overall strategies (more on that in the next two chapters).[1]

Algorithmic pandering makes slang terms inextricable from the metadata that help them spread. As early as the summer of 2023, people were making "rizz" content because the keyword "rizz" was trending, and the keyword "rizz" was trending because the algorithm decided that it would be so. I call this the *engagement treadmill*. As certain types of content get engagement, more creators make those types of videos, so more people engage with it, so more creators make it.

Each individual word in the Rizzler song went through this cycle. They were already trending keywords before the meme went viral, and then they became even trendier afterward.

Social media platforms reward using keywords because they want the information: Metadata can be turned into index terms that are easier for the algorithm to categorize, and thus know what to recommend to viewers. Creators want their content to be discoverable, so they mold it around what the algorithm wants. Keywords are a win-win.

........

The impact of the Rizzler song, and its subsequent spin-offs, cannot be overstated. It defined a pivotal turning point in the social media zeitgeist. It spawned an entire genre of "brainrot" comedy that redefined how we talk about social media and language. Most important, it gave its words a platform to spread— and spread they did. Three months after the song came out, I surveyed seventeen hundred middle school teachers and parents about these words. Fifty-five percent reported hearing their kids say "gyat," and 80 percent had heard the word "rizz,"* which became so popular that the *Oxford English Dictionary* chose it as its 2023 Word of the Year. A year later, and you couldn't find a middle-schooler who didn't know these two words. All the Rizzler slang terms had reached a point where they were being used regularly and unironically by Gen Alpha children, who had gotten them straight from short-video sites like TikTok and YouTube Shorts.

The Rizzler song is also emblematic of the post-Vine era of etymology—a time when language change is more overtly tied to viral memes, when trending words are more frequently replicated in new contexts. After the initial audio did the rounds, the original meme died out, but the words were still trendy, so creators found creative ways to replicate them through new formats. Some of the words, for example, took on an additional expletive function, as in the popular interjections "what the sigma" or "on skibidi."

Here, "sigma" and "skibidi" replace the words "fuck" and "God,"** but they also fit into what we call *phrasal templates*— familiar, repeatable phrases where any word can be inserted into a sort of verbal formula. For "on skibidi," the word "skibidi" fits into the phrasal template "on *X*," where an oath can be sworn on any noun. In the past, these oaths were often serious (you might sub in "my dead grandmother" or something similarly macabre), but the template has since expanded to include humorous words: Around the time that "on skibidi" was trending, it would also not be out of place to see the phrases "on sigma" or "on gyat."

As ridiculous as those examples seem, phrasal templates are nothing new. You already use them every day. The template "*X* is the new *Y*" is a sentence format where you can insert any two words to indicate a successive relationship (a famous example

---

* The real numbers are probably much higher, since parents are always out of the loop.
** Drawing on the Gen Z slang expression "on god."

being *Orange Is the New Black*), but that's just an easy-to-point-to example. These kinds of grammatical skeletons shape a huge portion of our conversations, and it's simply easier to fit our words around linguistic archetypes we're familiar with.

Likewise, there's a certain humor in applying new words to existing phrasal templates. That's why replacing "fuck" with "sigma" sounded so funny to the people who were saying "what the sigma." That's why other phrasal templates are so widespread. The format "she *X* on my *Y* till I *Z*" is seen as funny with pretty much any substitution, so we got sentences like "she rizz on my gyat till I ohio." It's mostly nonsensical, yes, but the value of these templates and the way they can be combined with each other allows the words to stay in circulation much longer than they would otherwise. Each reiteration lengthens the lifespan of the term, outliving the initial meme while retaining an original feel.

It's also just a fun opportunity to goof around with grammar. The British linguist David Crystal argues that this type of "language play" helps with language development in children and gives us more ways to express ourselves. Essentially, we're stimulating our brains by playing Mad Libs through our slang words, so it's not necessarily a bad thing if your middle school kid comes home saying something like "I went to gyatville and everyone knew you," drawing on a popular template of "going to *X*-ville."

In the past, phrasal templates existed only as particularly catchy turns of phrase. They were still structures for words to spread, but the internet took them to a completely new level through meme culture, building our humor out of easily combined patterns of mutual references.

Tellingly, these patterns are called *meme templates*. Whenever an image or video is accompanied by a caption, that caption uses some kind of phrasal template to convey a humorous idea, drawing on a shared knowledge of that format. These are often instrumental in spreading modern slang. Look at the word "function" becoming a synonym of "party"* in 2023: The shift entirely happened because of meme templates like "White people when there's *X* at the function," later evolving into "When the function has *X*." Both formats relied on the creative motivations people had for attending parties, and both relied on "function" as a contextually humorous word. Since the jokes were funny, the meme templates spread, and the meaning of "function" changed.

. . . . . . . .

It isn't new for slang to spread with memes. We've already learned how the word "okay" became popular through what was essentially a meme fad in Boston newspapers. People have always been using words and phrasal templates that they find funny.

Despite this, it's hard to pinpoint what exactly a meme *is*. The modern concept of a "self-replicating unit of culture" traces back to the 1976 Richard Dawkins book, *The Selfish Gene,* but the label has since been applied to various definitions across disciplines. Most interpretations agree that it's a type of idea characterized by its ability to spread between people.

Memes have always been kind of like a virus. Whenever you learn a new word, you can think of it as coming into contact with a parasite. Either your guard is up and you reject the word, or it breaks through your defenses and you become a "host," using and replicating the word for it to reach a larger population. Then there's the uncanny similarity between how we talk about the ways that words and diseases spread: We say they move through social networks in a "viral" manner, hence the phrase "gone viral." Many linguists even use epidemiological models to show the spread or lifespan of ideas.[2]

---

* The word previously had an association with formal events, but only recently came to be associated with drunken college ragers.

Just like viruses, memes compete against each other in the wild. In the days of Vine, for instance, the funniest or catchiest meme would receive the most "likes" and then rise up higher in a user's feed, thus reaching a larger audience because it was more "evolutionarily fit" to spread. If the meme was replicable, it would survive longer in our collective consciousness, like with the various "yeet" meme formats.

Since then, however, the qualifications for an evolutionarily "fit" meme have changed with algorithmic video recommendations. The new social media platforms are more deliberate about keeping users engaged as long as possible, and now reward a new host of metrics for creators to optimize for. A "fit" or "viral" video needs so much more than just "likes"; it needs a long average watch time, a lot of comments, and a lot of shares, in addition to all the other constraints of the algorithm.

Arguably, slang words—already inextricable from their metadata—have also become inextricable from memes. The word "sigma" became popular through the sigma meme templates, and the sigma meme templates became popular because the algorithm rewarded content containing that word. TikTok knew that the people liked sigma content, because it consistently generated more interactions than other words for "successful male." As a result, "sigma" assumed a more prominent position in our slang, outcompeting potential synonyms. Its funniness made it catchy, which is probably why so many algospeak words like "seggs" and "nip nops" also sound a little funny, or why we immediately think of memes as funny ideas.

Importantly for its success, "sigma" was an easily replicable meme. The fact that it could be recombined into templates like "what the sigma" and "on sigma" meant that it could be used and applied in more contexts than just the original joke, giving it more opportunities to "infect hosts" and help the "virus" survive. Same thing with "side-eye": New trends give words the ability to outlast the previous meme's lifespan.

Linguists have known for a while that words are more likely to succeed if they appear in many grammatical situations. If a slang term shows up across multiple phrasal templates and linguistic contexts, it's more likely that it'll stick around in at least one of those templates or contexts. Modern memes give us a new lens to consider this. Words can now also reproduce if we adapt them to different trends and meme templates—all of which are spread by the algorithm.

At its core, our "modern slang" is spreading exactly as our "old slang" did, only through a new medium. Before the internet, ideas would move across geographic territory between people in similar social circles. Now the various corners of social media have replaced physical territory, but individual words will still spread between people in the same "social networks." There's still regional variation—people will talk distinctly on different platforms or in different online communities—and new slang still shocks people when it subverts a "standard dialect" (which is why the Rizzler song was so effective in capturing our attention).

However, the role of "slang" in popular culture has fundamentally changed because of the internet. Since the emergence of Standard English, the rule makers of language have been in charge, and their prescriptive norms about a "correct" version of the English language have dominated our channels of communication. If you wanted your voice to be heard by the public, you had to work within their constraints, conforming to the stringent expectations of either print or broadcast media.

Social media completely shattered that barrier. The playing field is now level, and public access is democratized. Anybody and everybody can become a public figure on the new communicative platforms, meaning that nobody's left to enforce the old rules. TV presenters and journalists might not have been able to use slang, but content creators can. We regularly use words like "function" and "side-eye," and our influence both legitimizes these terms and gives them a large platform to spread quicker than they could have before.

Content creators also come from a greater variety of backgrounds than people working in traditional media. This means that slang can more naturally transcend the economic and social barriers that once hampered its growth. Black and queer people, for example, have a larger voice than ever before, meaning that Black and queer slang has diffused into the popular vernacular with unprecedented speed. The loose social networks that previously connected us geographically are simply stronger online, and memes are now transmitted at breakneck pace.

If you're taking notes, you'll notice the definition of "slang" has subtly changed since the start of this chapter. In the eighteenth century, the word was very intentionally targeted toward the language of the lower classes. The elitism is still there—that's why we disproportionately talk about "slang" when it's being used by minority communities—but now you'd be hard-pressed to find someone who doesn't admit to using slang occasionally; now the term simply refers to "informal speech" in general. Everybody speaks informally, especially because everybody participates in the social media sociolect. We just understand it's something to code-switch in and out of, which is why we mark off words as "internet slang" or "Gen Z slang."

. . . . . . . .

In September 2021, the TikToker Anthony Mai posted a video urging his followers to participate in a prank: For no reason, everybody should suddenly start commenting the chair emoji (🪑) in lieu of the laughing emoji for all videos by KSI, another social media influencer. The video went extremely viral, and for the next few weeks it seemed as if everybody on TikTok was spamming 🪑 in not only KSI's comments but under every successful video. Google searches for "chair emoji meaning" spiked, and people began speculating whether the emoji had officially become the new laughing emoji.

Within a month, however, the chair emoji virtually disappeared online. Search trends came crashing back down, and by November almost everybody had forgotten about the fad. It was yet another ephemerality briefly occupying the incessantly mesmerizing carousel of trends, memes, and emojis that constantly grip the social media space.

Why, though? Why did 🪑 die out, while the laughing-crying emoji came back in full force? What causes a word or meme to fizzle out, while others stay around for much longer?

The American sociologist Everett Rogers attempts to answer this question in his 1962 book, *Diffusion of Innovations*. In it, he breaks down how all information moves across five categories of "adopters":

1. The innovators—a small group of people, like Anthony, who are willing to take risks by coming up with new ideas.
2. The early adopters—people comfortable with adopting new ideas, who don't take much convincing. In this case, Anthony's followers.
3. The early majority—people willing to hop onto a trend once they see it taking off among a small group.
4. The late majority—those who adopt a trend once they see the majority using it. Once this group started using the chair, it really started showing up everywhere.
5. The laggards—the last people to adopt an idea; the ones who had to google "what does the chair emoji mean?"[3]

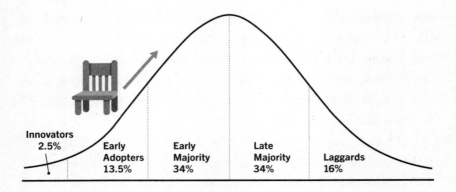

"Adoption" doesn't mean that the word is around to stay. After someone makes the initial decision to start incorporating a slang term into their vocabulary, they later make another decision either to continue using the term or to abandon it. This is often sociologically conditioned: As soon as the laggards start using a word, the innovators and early adopters will either begin to see it as uncool or find a permanent use for it (after which the rest of the population will follow). In the case of the 🪑 emoji, its initial appeal was that it was part of an in-joke. Once everybody caught up, it lost its value, and there was no particular reason to keep it around.

Curiously, around the same time, the skull emoji (💀) began to widely replace the laughing-crying emoji as the preferred Gen Z expression of humor, through the idea of being "dead" from laughing. By the end of 2022, even the laggards on TikTok were socially pressured into using the emoji, but the key difference is that it didn't die out like 🪑. After the adopters reached critical mass, they chose to keep it around, because it served an important purpose differentiating them from older generations who still predominantly used the 😂 emoji for laughing online.

There are a few reasons why one meme might survive while another fails to stick the landing. It all comes down to what Everett calls the "innovation-decision process": whether the adopters decide to continue or stop using an idea. This is influenced by a number of inter- and intrapersonal factors.

One of these factors is *frequency*: Is the term culturally trending? Humans are social creatures who adopt words if they have a social purpose. Both 🪑 and 💀 had a social purpose as cultural references to bond over, even if 💀 trended more in the long run. Once people see other people use a word, they want to be in on the reference and use the word themselves. This means that a word can continue trending simply because it was trending in the first place, and we've already learned how social media really accelerates this into a positive feedback loop.

It's also important for a word to be *unobtrusive,* meaning that it shouldn't feel too noticeable or forced. As entertaining as the 🪑 meme was, it never really had a chance because people knew it was artificial. The entire joke revolved around the fact that it was an unnatural way to express laughter, and once the joke was over, it stuck out like a sore thumb.

Although the chair emoji was an extreme example, obtrusiveness will always kill a word in the end. That's why we no longer say "yeet" or "on fleek." The words stuck out as examples of "Gen Z slang," and thus were tied to our expectations about what "slang" is. Once the laggards (that is, millennials and Gen X parents) started saying the words, they rapidly lost their cool factor and were quickly replaced by other funny interjections and adjectives.

Meanwhile, consider the word "cancel," which began to take on a definition of "socially ostracize" around the same time as the word "yeet" got popular. "Cancel" was also "Gen Z slang," but it wasn't thought of as such. Instead, it was an unobtrusive word. Nobody noticed it entering our vocabulary; it felt quite natural, as if it had always been there. By the time the laggards began using the word, it didn't feel surprising or alienating.

Whenever people make fun of the "Gen Z slang" or "Gen

Alpha slang" being spread on TikTok, they usually point to obtrusive words. It's much easier to notice ridiculous-sounding words like "gyat" and "skibidi," but those never had staying power because they were far too in-your-face about it. Slang terms like "function" and "side-eye," however, are much more likely to fly under the radar, because they consist of already familiar words and are remarked on much less frequently. A good rule of thumb is that if someone can make fun of you for saying something, it's probably obtrusive. That's why Gretchen couldn't make "fetch" happen in *Mean Girls:* It was too noticeable.

Paradoxically, memes help words spread, but if a word is *too* tied to a meme, it attracts attention and becomes obtrusive. Trends in general are a double-edged sword: They bring slang terms to prominence, but their transience can sabotage those terms' success. If an idea is overly tied to a fad, it'll die with that fad, unless it can find a way to jump between many different grammatical and social situations. The algorithm doesn't care. It'll just amplify the next trend—whatever it takes to keep the masses entertained.

At the same time, the more memes a word can hop between, the better chance it has for survival, because it's generating more potential opportunities to survive. Even if a word has both high frequency and low obtrusiveness, it needs a reason to be used, known as an *endurance* factor. That's why phrasal templates are so important: They give words different contexts to appear in.

In the end, a word will stick if it serves a new role in the English language. If, as with "cancel," it defines a necessary concept, then we say that it's filled a *semantic gap:* a concept that we didn't previously have a word for. Had there already been an entrenched word for the same idea, we would have had no need to cancel people. Sometimes, though, the new word also provides a better or funnier way to express a concept than existing synonyms, which is why "function" was able to slowly start supplanting "party": It filled the semantic gap of a silly way to talk about social events.[4]

It's pointless trying to predict which individual slang words will succeed and which will fail. Language is a chaotic, entropic thing with too many variables at play, and we can only really identify correlations.

What we do know, however, is that memes are more than jokes: They're conveyors of culture. Their influence, now adapted to short-form video platforms, isn't going anywhere. Nor are the platforms. Between TikTok, Instagram Reels, YouTube Shorts, and other apps like Douyin or Xiaohongshu, social media companies have cracked the formula for your attention. With every swipe, you unlock another hit of dopamine, and it's all too easy to immerse yourself in a highly personalized stream of entertainment. Until a more addicting media format is invented, these apps will continue their stranglehold on how we communicate, thereby influencing the language we use.

Words, which have always been tied to trends, are only going to continue being pushed by algorithms engineered to reward those trends. The old boundary between slang and "proper speech" has been dissolved and redefined. Now all slang terms have a new avenue for spreading to a larger audience than ever before, faster than ever before.

Memes, meanings, and metadata are one and the same, building up our vocabulary through humor and hashtags. And, as you'll find out in the next chapter, the name of this game is your attention.

# No Because What Happened
# to Your Attention?

BACK IN HIGH SCHOOL, well before I ever thought I'd be earning a living as a content creator, I had a fairly successful stint as a Reddit influencer. Every morning, I would wake up, post, and comment across the most popular subreddits—getting that rush of dopamine whenever I'd check back to see that thousands of people had upvoted my latest content. By my senior year, I was one of the top 80 users on a website of 330 million people. I was utterly hooked. It was an exhilarating, addicting distraction from the intense stress of the college application cycle.

Beyond that, though, I think I was drawn to Reddit because it presented a social puzzle. Each post was an opportunity to explore the mass psyche, to see whether I knew how to properly capture people's attention. To go viral, I simply had to outcompete other posts by gaming what I knew about psychology and social media dynamics.

Thankfully, Reddit made this extremely easy by making its source code publicly available. Anyone trying to make their content seen by a lot of people just had to play within a specific post-ranking algorithm:[1]

$$s_{jt} = \text{sign}\left(u_{jt}\right)\log_{10}\left(\max\left\{|u_{jt}|, 1\right\}\right) - \frac{a_{jt}}{45,000}$$

While this formula might seem complicated at first glance, it was, in fact, extraordinarily simple compared with the sophisticated recommendation systems you're now familiar with. Much like on Vine, machine learning algorithms had nothing to do with a post's popularity. Instead, the only variables were $u$, the number of upvotes minus the number of downvotes, and $a$, the age of the post. Whatever the output was (here represented by $s$) determined how high a post would rank relative to other posts.

To make a post go viral, then, I just had to find something people would upvote and post it at the right time in the right subreddit—usually when an older post's ranking was decaying due to the age variable. That's why I would usually post in the morning: Most people don't start posting until later in the day, so my content would rank better against the aging submissions from the previous day and get a lot of early upvotes.

After enough practice, the variable $a$ grew to feel so predictable that my only real challenge was $u$: getting my posts upvoted. Part of this hinged on finding ideas that would be socially successful—I usually focused on feel-good or interesting educational content—but the other part was framing them the right way. Oftentimes, this would differ across subreddits, but all of it would rely on manipulating people's attention. Over time, I learned to very carefully phrase my post captions to maximize your curiosity. I noticed that it worked best when a title was moderately descriptive, drawing you in while leaving you curious for more.

To corroborate my experiences, I reached out to Shriya Mandal, a friend of mine who peaked at No. 11 on the Reddit leaderboard around the same time when I was active. She was similarly analytical in her approach, noting that you have only "a split second to make someone look at your post, [so] the title is super important." Too short, and it's not interesting: People don't want to look at a picture just titled "snow," because that just sounds generic. Too long, on the other hand, and people don't want to waste time reading it. Instead, Shriya would give her posts titles like "Snowfall in Sequoia National Park, California," because that's just enough to succinctly capture the viewer's curiosity and lure them in.

That kind of title might not seem remarkable to you, but the wording works wonders because it falls into a marketing Goldilocks zone called the *curiosity gap*. You know what snow looks like, but you don't know what snow in Sequoia National Park looks like, so you become slightly more curious. You've suddenly discovered a gap in your knowledge that you need to fill.

Both of us also noticed that viewers respond well to emotional language. One of Shriya's top posts is titled "This athlete with cerebral palsy deadlifted 200lb at 99lb." The caption still satisfies a curiosity gap (you know what deadlifting looks like; you don't know what it looks like when a CP patient does it), but it additionally exploits a sense of sympathy for the athlete. Shriya is sure that the post wouldn't have done nearly as well if she hadn't mentioned the words "cerebral palsy." Perhaps that goes without saying, for this is an extreme example, but there are many, more subtle ways to affect emotion that creators must constantly think about. If we can somehow make you connect with our content, you're more likely to upvote it. This isn't limited to post titles. We'll find and use whatever linguistic tricks we can to get your attention and go viral, which will often end up changing *everybody's* language as a result.

. . . . . . . .

The fact that we could see and learn from Reddit's algorithm was a fleeting rarity in the late 2010s. Social media companies have very little incentive to release their source code, out of both intellectual property concerns and a fear that their competitors will build a better version of their technology. Reddit started out as more of a democratic social media experiment, but as it got bigger, it ran into the same problems and diverged from its original mission. By 2017, it also had made its algorithm secret, and it's clear from looking at your home page that it has also started using AI to personalize recommendations. Posts don't show up in the formulaic way they used to; rather, there's a far more mysterious set of rules governing your feed. On other platforms, it's even more haphazard: Posting time, for example, seems to matter much less on apps like TikTok.

The underlying strategies, however, remain the same. Influencers are still trying to create content that will emotionally or linguistically resonate with people, because that generates increased interaction in a way that'll be amplified by the platform and help their posts go viral. The strategies for post captions almost perfectly translate over to the short-form video era. For example, I'm forced to think how to frame early on-screen text in a way that will make people want to continue watching my entire video.

At the same time, I now also have to carefully consider the first few words I say out loud. How can I best interrupt someone's scrolling pattern and persuade them to listen to what I have to say? As Shriya pointed out, I have only a split second to work with, so everything matters.

This is where emotion comes in handy. One of the most common influencer tactics is to employ superlatives, or extreme language, in our video hooks. Here are some that I've personally used in my most viral videos:

- My **favorite** thing about $X$ is . . .
- This is my **least favorite** thing about $X$.
- I am **constantly amazed** by $X$.
- The **most interesting** $X$ is . . .
- The **best** part of $X$ is . . .
- It should be **illegal** to $X$.
- I **hate it more than anything** when $X$ . . .

All these opening lines work because they're bold claims. There are so many interesting things out there, but only one thing could be the *most interesting*. As the viewer, you're now intrigued: How will I as the influencer defend my outlandish statement? The only way to find out is to keep watching, which is exactly what I want you to do.

These are also inherently emotional statements. By saying that something is the "most interesting," I'm connecting the statement to my intense personal opinions, which makes you invested. Humans are empathetic creatures; you resonate more when someone is expressing their extreme emotions.

Psychologists have known about the relationship between emotional content and virality since at least 2010, when two Wharton professors found that emotionally charged *New York Times* articles were far more likely to be shared over email than emotionally neutral articles. It mattered less whether the content was positive or negative, only that it had high "content valence"— that it expressed extreme emotion in either direction.[2]

Since the Wharton paper, these results have been replicated across a wide variety of media and connected more explicitly to social media virality: A 2020 NYU study also found that greater emotional connection influenced user participation and sharing behaviors on Twitter. One can see, then, how influencers might be incentivized to use extreme language on short-form video platforms that highly reward those metrics.[3]

Of course, most influencers aren't basing their content choices on academic research: We instead learn from watching the same pattern play out in our video analytics. I can see the exact time stamps when people stop watching my posts, and by comparing how people respond to my language choices across many different videos, I've noticed a trend that superlative-laden hooks retain audiences more than emotionally neutral equivalents. Most creators likely figure it out the same way, or they just stumble on a format that works through trial and error. Many of the successful creators I've studied rotate between a few set opening lines. They know exactly what they're doing, and that's just one trick in their arsenal.

Another classic strategy is to use second-person pronouns as much as possible, because you're selfish. You connect more to content that's about you, since you can better identify with it. Here are some more hooks I've used successfully:

- If **you're** looking for *X*, then *Y*.
- **You** know how *X*?
- I'm sure **you've** heard *X*.
- I'm gonna need to put **you** onto *X*.
- If **you** do *X*, this is how **you** *Y*.
- **You** should stop doing *X*.
- Have **you** noticed *X*?

Again, there's a psychological explanation for why these openers work: The word "you" frames what I'm going to say in a way that will make you connect it to your life experiences. Consider the following two hooks:

*This is how influencers make videos.*
*This is how **you** can make videos like an influencer.*

The first hook seems detached because I've abstracted my explanation to the third person. The second hook, however, encourages you to build a narrative around my words. Even if you don't want to be an influencer, you're now putting yourself in the shoes of one. You've become personally invested in what I have to say, which was my goal. Now you're more likely to watch past the first few seconds, helping my video perform better in the algorithm.

This phenomenon isn't restricted to social media. Research has found that songs on the *Billboard* charts tend to be more liked and more purchased if they use more second-person pronouns, due to the fact that they "facilitate feelings of social connection." Words make it easier for us to map our experiences onto others.[4]

They can also foster parasocial interactions. By personalizing my video with familiar pronouns, I'm tricking you into feeling as though we have a two-way connection. I'm incentivized to do this because you're more likely to interact with my videos if you feel some kind of individual relationship to me.

However, I don't even have to use the word "you" to make you feel as if you were involved. I can instead leverage group dynamics:

- I can't be the **only one** who's noticed X.
- Am I the **only one** who didn't know X?

If you *did* notice or know the thing I'm talking about, you feel good about yourself because you're part of an in-group; you feel included. If you *didn't*, then you start to feel left out of a social experience. Lucky for you, the way to become part of the in-group is to watch my video. I can also more deliberately play into this feeling through the following lines:

- **People** are finally doing *X*.
- One thing **people** don't tell you about *X* is *Y*.
- Why aren't **people** talking about *X*?
- I don't think **people** understand/realize *X*.

Once more, if you're part of "people," you're going to feel connected to my topic. If you're not part of "people," you now want to catch up, or else you run the risk of being behind on a cultural reference or piece of information. My job as a creator is to understand this. I must figure out how to grab your attention and use the specific language that's best for doing that.

· · · · · · · ·

It's an unfortunate reality that all influencers somehow manipulate your emotions to go viral, since we're all competing for your attention, and we know that your attention is tied to your emotions. Personally, I've always felt a mild cognitive dissonance about this, but I try to justify it by providing well-researched and high-quality content. Even though I have to work within the constraints of social media, I try to do so conscientiously.

Other creators have fewer reservations, and will intentionally lean into incendiary or frustrating language to steal your attention. This strategy, called *ragebaiting,* has long been a well-known tactic in mainstream media: Before Tucker Carlson's show was canceled in 2023, he notably amassed one of the largest audiences in television history through frequent use of hyperbole and outraged rhetoric. Tucker knew that his viewership would grow every time he provoked feelings of anger, so he routinely ragebaited to increase his relevance.

Since the rise of social media, however, the ragebait phenom-enon has become widespread among everyday creators. In some cases, it's spawned reliable income streams and even careers, such as with the actress Louisa Melcher, who built up an audi-ence of nearly a million followers by posting elaborate lies on TikTok. Each video is more outrageous than the next: In one, she pretends to be a roller skater who fell offstage at the Super Bowl halftime show, while in the next she claims that she will be the first solo passenger to be launched into a one-way space mission. All are absurd fabrications, but each video generates consistent engagement from viewers who may or may not real-ize they've been misled.

When I reached out to interview Louisa for this book, I was surprised by how systematic she also was about her videos. She saw her content as a form of "performance art," with complex motivations, and virality was part of the act. Yes, she wanted to promote herself as an artist, but she also took joy in reflect-ing society back to itself, satirizing the social media experience through deliberately sparking intense emotions.

To my further fascination, Louisa then went on to mention the exact same interest in group behavior that initially drew me to post on Reddit. Each video was a "personally fulfilling chal-lenge" for her to predict "what's going to inspire the strongest reaction." It was a chance to better understand "what makes people tick." Knowing how to capture attention is far more important than knowing the algorithm; algorithms change, but the things that interest us remain the same. "If there's one fun-damental feature I expect will never change," Louisa tells me, "it's that content that elicits a strong response will be pushed to more viewers." As such, she optimizes for maximally hyperbolic hooks—whatever it takes to keep "eyes on the video."

You'll notice that Louisa's hook strategies aren't that different from my own. She'll often use superlatives and frequently start her videos by implying that *everyone* has already seen something (her roller-skating video starts out with the sentence "I've been seeing all your guys' memes," suggesting that her accident was a popular occurrence and encouraging the viewer to keep watching, "since no one wants to be out of the loop"). Whether the viewer does or doesn't believe the ultimate story, they are nevertheless driven to comment on their emotional response, which of course drives engagement on the app.

Louisa's content is notable not only because it angers her audience but also because it captivates them. Her opening lines are so sensational that you're drawn to watch her videos even if you know they're fake. At a certain point, her ragebaiting becomes indistinguishable from another phenomenon: clickbaiting, or the attraction of attention through (often deceptively) enticing promises.

Although Louisa's video hooks click-bait the viewer using the promise of a crazy story, video clickbait can be far more obvious. I've frequently been frustrated by a creator claiming to have "the eighth greatest fact of all time" and then explaining the (frequently misleading) fact without ever revealing why it's the eighth greatest. Nevertheless, I feel compelled to watch the video because I want to know *why* it's the eighth greatest fact. It's like those BuzzFeed articles claiming that the ninth fact on their list will surprise you. These content styles exploit our curiosity gap between knowing that facts exist and not knowing why some facts are better than others, yet they regularly withhold that satisfaction, which helpfully spurs comments of frustration.

Whenever I watch the eighth-greatest-fact videos, I know I'll eventually be disappointed. Paradoxically, I keep "hate-watching" them anyway out of a sense of spite. I'm not alone in this: Look at shows like *Riverdale* and *Too Hot to Handle,* which were universally panned as "trashy" and yet are still watched by hundreds of millions. It feels good to criticize something when it makes us feel better about ourselves. Whether it's an obnoxious Netflix show or a stupid TikTok, it can be a guilty pleasure to feel a little self-righteous. Ironically, we're feeding into the system we love to hate: Whenever ragebait content successfully goads us into engaging with it, the algorithm pushes more ragebait content as a good way to keep people on the app.

Admittedly, the "eighth greatest fact" videos aren't too abrupt of a departure from my claims that something is the "most interesting thing about X." There's still an element of exaggeration, though I'd argue that the former takes it too far, capitalizing on your attention by overly playing into a sense of theatricality. Either way, it's nothing new. Well before people like Tucker Carlson, this particular tactic has actually been commonplace in media since the "yellow journalism" of the late nineteenth century. In a bid to steal readership from competing papers, newspapers intentionally printed hyperbolized, emotional headlines—effectively boosting their reach by click-baiting and ragebaiting the American population.

· · · · · · · ·

I've always found it fascinating that we talk about attention as something that is "captured" and "held" before eventually being "lost." To be *captivating*, something must hold you *captive*, the implication being that your attention was seized and could escape at any moment. There's a sense of scarcity, of ephemerality, and in the internet age there's a real pressure on those who want to hold your easily fractured attention.

In 1971, the Nobel Prize–winning political scientist Herbert A. Simon coined the phrase "attention economy" to describe this phenomenon. In his view, attention was a limited resource to be allocated among competing stimuli in an information-rich environment. Since then, the concept* has been extended to numerous applications in marketing and psychology,[5] but the most salient example is in social media. As soon as a video bores you, a quick flick of the finger will send it into oblivion, instantly conjuring up a new video to entertain you instead. That means that influencers are quite literally competing with each other for your attention. The second your mind starts to wander, you scroll. This hurts our *retention rate,* a measurement of how long people watch our videos, and retention rate is a critical factor in those videos being promoted by the algorithm (built to keep people on the app for as long as possible). Hence, if a video is bad at getting your attention, it won't even be recommended to you in the first place.

Attention is always important if you want to share a message, but the way to hold it changes across mediums. If I'm delivering a speech to an auditorium of people, I don't have to rely on the same tricks as I do online. I have them *captive:* They can't scroll away. Same with books. I had to draw you in with a flashy jacket or interesting description, but now that you're reading, I have access to a different, longer kind of attention where I can lend nuance to my opinions without the fear that you'll immediately put this down for another book the moment I write a lackluster sentence.

Things are different online, where I feel like I'm fighting a constant war for your attention. I carefully script out all my videos to maximize the addictiveness of each sentence. Beyond the initial hook, I sneak in little "microhooks" to everything I say, making sure I recapture your attention if it does happen to drift. Even my content choices and presentation styles are subordinated to the pressures of social media. No matter how interesting I find the etymology of the word "concept," I know that a

---

* Another word coming from the Latin word for "to take," implying that you *take in* a concept. Think about how we talk about "grasping" a concept today.

video on "skibidi toilet" will do better, because of the way that the algorithm amplifies trends.

Even when I did make a video on the etymology of "skibidi," I ragebaited my audience to a certain extent. I knew some people would be upset about the latest generational slang, which would make them hate-watch and comment. For those who liked consuming skibidi content, it instead click-baited them, by framing the video as a form of entertainment that they had reliably enjoyed in the past. All this played further into an ongoing social trend, since I knew people were fascinated by that word at the time.

In fact, failure to adapt to trends is an incredibly dangerous pitfall for influencers. It's very easy to lose touch with the ever-changing algorithm unless you're constantly keeping your finger on the pulse. I have several good friends who racked up millions of followers in the early days of social media, but are unable to get more than a few thousand views on their videos today because they either took a break or didn't keep up with the changing times. In my first year on TikTok alone, I watched the platform slowly break free from its short Vine-like style as the algorithm began pushing videos over a minute in length. This was a deliberate decision by ByteDance to begin chipping away at YouTube's monopoly on long-form video, and if I hadn't responded by switching to longer-form videos, my TikToks would have received progressively fewer views until I potentially lost my audience entirely. Remember that the algorithm reflects the creative direction of social media companies. Not conforming or simply not being aware of those directions results in your content performing worse.

I experienced this firsthand on Reddit. Since its algorithm switched away from the simple 2016 formula to its current recommendation-based AI system, I've found that I've completely lost the ability to understand what will do well on the website. My etymology infographics, which would easily get tens of thousands of upvotes when I was familiar with the post-ranking methodology, now flounder in the hundreds. The artistic and educational quality of my content hasn't declined, but the algorithm is now rewarding new metrics and it seems I'm out of touch.

All this reinforces the notion that creators must mold ourselves to the algorithm to have the best chance at capturing your attention. Some linguistic techniques, like the superlatives or second-person pronouns, stay fairly constant. We often figure these out through trial and error or by looking at our video analytics. Other techniques, like use of the word "skibidi," fluctuate with the algorithm, and we hop onto them by observing other popular videos, then replicating them in our own way.

In many cases, creators are additionally incentivized to come up with their own catchy terms or phrases, since they can grab people's attention and spawn interaction. Along the lines of clickbait or ragebait, this growing phenomenon is specifically described as *trendbait*—saying things specifically in the hopes of becoming a viral trend. A prototypical example is "girl dinner," coined by the TikToker Olivia Maher to describe a humorously unhealthy replacement for a formal meal. Following Olivia's video, it became a viral trend for girls to talk about their own version of "girl dinner." Many of these reactions took the form of comments or "stitches," generating more engagement and relevance for Olivia. At a certain point, a "girl dinner" song was written, and the meme took on a second life, but anyone curious about the origin of the trend could go back and rewatch the first video, presumably earning Olivia more income with each view.

I've also done this: In early 2024, I went viral for talking about the "boomer ellipses," a phrase I coined to describe how older people use different punctuation in their messages. Since I said the phrase confidently, but nobody knew it at the time, the wording drew in more people wanting to know about a phenomenon they thought they had somehow missed out on. Similar phrases go viral every week whenever creators try to start a new trend, from "Roman Empire" to "beige flag" to "orange peel theory" (if you're unfamiliar with these, congrats for not being chronically online in 2023).

Even without an explicit effort to "trendbait," creators know that using certain phrases will help their video do better. In one of my viral etymology videos, for example, I explained how the adverb "lowkey" functions "kinda like the word kinda, or sorta like the word sorta." I specifically scripted out the phrase like that because I knew it would generate interaction, and it did: Hundreds of people ended up commenting on the wordplay, boosting my video in the algorithm and helping me rack up more than three million views across platforms. I've similarly noticed many other creators successfully use clever turns of phrase online, simply because we know it works.

In one viral video, the TikTok creator Khai Bellamy recounts the story of how her dad persuaded her family to fly on a budget airline. It's an otherwise normal story, but Khai's word choice drives it home. Each sentence would function as an amazingly wry one-liner, from describing the plane as "a closet with wings" run by "Kendall Jenner airlines" to talking about how her family subsequently "Amish shunned" her dad while her mom put him on "marital probation." Khai, who has amassed more than 2.6 million followers for her addictively engaging story-time videos, tells me that this is very much intentional. Before filming a video, she thinks of certain jokes or analogies she knows she wants to include, since wordplay captures viewers' attention and consistently generates comments from people quoting their favorite part of the video. She also sees it as a way to keep the video "fluid, fun, and engaging," which helps with viewer retention.

Evidently, it pays to experiment linguistically. In some cases, like with "Roman Empire," these experiments worm their way into our lexicon before anyone notices. This happens much more frequently than you might expect: Much of our new slang is emerging from people finding something catchy online. I've watched many of my friends criticize each other for "talking like TikTok," referring to a slew of grammatical constructions popularized as meme-based phrasal templates online:

- *It's giving ____*
- *It's the ____ for me*
- *The way you ____*
- *Not you doing ____*

These sentence formats* have spread beyond social media because there's something underlyingly catchy about them. Certain turns of phrase are more distinctive than others, in a way that's psychologically satisfying to us. These phrasal templates intrigued us, first in the online space and then eventually offline once they were repeated enough by others around us.

Even individual words like "skibidi" and "side-eye" need to bait you somehow if they are to become viral. It doesn't matter what kind of bait is used or what psychological appeal it uses. If this is a fishing metaphor, the way I reel you in is first by hooking your attention.

. . . . . . . .

After TikTok hit the scene, a new grammatical construction rapidly became popular among younger generations: the interjection "no because."** Rather than indicating opposition to

---

\* Again, borrowed from African American English.
\*\* Heard in the classroom by 60 percent of the middle school teachers I surveyed in March 2024.

something, as you might expect from the word "no," the phrase is used to introduce a sentence, generally to add emphasis. Here's an example:

> **No because** *when did everybody start saying "no because"?*

At face value, the "no" and "because" seem completely unprompted and unnecessary to the sentence. After all, the same meaning is communicated without those words, right?

Not exactly. "No because" serves two very important functions. First, it adds a tone of incredulity or excitement that would otherwise not be there. Second, it functions as a *discourse marker*—a phrase used to manage the flow of a conversation. Sociolinguistically speaking, that means that "no because" introduced my earlier sentence in the same way as the words "wait" or "hold on":

> **Wait,** *when did everybody start saying "no because"?*
> **Hold on,** *when did everybody start saying "no because"?*

In these sentences, the truth condition (underlying meaning) isn't affected by "wait" or "hold on." Instead, the discourse markers are used as little linguistic signals that the speaker is taking control of the discussion. They're subtle ways to communicate "look at me, it's my turn to speak," and that's exactly what's happening with "no because." It's a tactic used to gain attention.

Although discourse markers play an important role in managing turn-taking in real conversations, "no because" found the same purpose among content creators as all the other terms and phrases I've already mentioned. It's a way of interrupting your scrolling pattern, of signaling that you should pay attention *now*. And guess what? It works! At this point, the average social media user is conditioned to pause when they hear the words. They've previously introduced interesting videos, so there's a good reason to keep listening.

In psychology, this technique is called *priming*. When a person is exposed to a certain stimulus, they become more mentally prepared for a related stimulus. Over time, people have become "primed" to associate the "no because" discourse marker with engaging content. This effect is amplified by two factors: First, the people media-savvy enough to intentionally start their videos with a discourse marker are likely also good at making engaging videos, which suggests a real correlation with quality. Second, the more someone is taught to link two stimuli, the stronger the priming effect becomes, until "no because" eventually became a self-fulfilling prophecy.

We also have another important psychological function in play: *framing*. Since "no because" is typically deployed in exciting sentences, the discourse marker further serves to "frame" a viewer's perception of a video as interesting. Even before the influencer arrives at what they have to say, the viewer is already in a receptive headspace to hear a hot take or crazy story. It's kind of like how the word "you" frames a viewer's perception of a video by encouraging them to connect it to their personal experiences: "No because" sets their expectations to pay more attention to the content.

It's also just a confusing phrase. I like to think of "no because" as an attentional one-two punch: The "no" shocks you, and then the "because" reels you in to hear what the speaker actually has to say. Perhaps part of its widespread success can be attributed to the fact that it doesn't make that much intuitive sense. By the time your brain figures out what "no" could have been indicating opposition to, you've already been tricked into watching the rest of the video.

"No because" creates an interrupted, in medias res feel to its succeeding sentence, and that's great for social media. Viewers love abrupt, informal openings for the same reason that the technique has historically worked so well in literature and cinema: It throws you into a situation as if you were already there. An elaborate introduction would flop just as Shriya's Reddit post would have if it had contained more than a short sentence fragment about snow. Too much buildup fails to put us in the moment, thus failing to capture our attention.

Many influencers probably don't even realize they're saying "no because," but replicate the line because some part of them notices it perform successfully, or they see other influencers doing it. Keep in mind that anything showing up on your For You page is already successful, so a good tactic could unintentionally perpetuate itself: Ways of speaking may be normalized simply because they perform well.

The reason I find "no because" particularly compelling is that it appears to be a direct example of a social media attentional tactic seeping into our everyday conversation. I now regularly hear people saying "no because" in real life, and it's almost certainly due to TikTok. Of course, it's incredibly hard to prove causation between influencers saying a word and other people picking up that word; there's simply too much data to sift through and not enough evidence for *why* people start saying certain words. Theoretically, it could be the other way around: Influencers are saying it more because people are saying it more.

At the same time, the timing seems too convenient to ignore. If you look at Twitter search results for "no because" in 2019 (before it became popular on TikTok), the only people using it as an interjection are a few members of the Black community, where it originated.

Starting in 2020 (after "no because" became popular on TikTok), however, we begin seeing an increase in tweets using it as an interjection, especially among other races. Even if social media wasn't the only factor, the phrase at the very least simultaneously developed on- and offline, with the two environments influencing each other.

If anything, though, it's common sense that TikTok helped spread the phrase, for linguistic research has repeatedly proven that word acquisition is influenced by how frequently people see a word. Since TikTok's attention-based algorithm incentivizes frequent use of the phrase "no because," then, it's only logical that that would lead to more people using it in everyday conversation.

........

The connection between the internet and declining attention rates has long been studied and commented on. We know we're facing a full-blown social epidemic. People are reading less, students are struggling to remain on task, and we're all checking our phones way more than we should be. Even while writing this book, my "research" on TikTok has repeatedly devolved into scrolling as I quickly get sucked into the app's attention sinkhole. Nevertheless, I still find it shocking how easily this turns into a positive feedback loop. As our attention spans get shorter, advertisers and creators must compete harder for views, which leads to a constant and increasing bombardment of stimuli that ultimately causes our attention spans to decline further (and further escalates the competition).

It's a zero-sum game against every other creator on the app, and success can come down to the smallest details. Each additional attention-grabbing strategy exponentially contributes to a video's success. At a certain point, videos are recommended simply *because* they capture our attention. This is an online manifestation of a behavioral phenomenon called the *Matthew effect*: Essentially, content that is slightly better at capturing your attention will perform exponentially better on social media.

Part of this is a normal mathematical principle of virality. If a post is shared 20 percent less, it's going to be seen not by 20 percent fewer people but by *90 percent* fewer, because fewer people will even be given the chance to share it in the first place.[6] On video platforms, this 20 percent difference determines whether a video gets a hundred thousand or a million views, and that's before we consider human behavior in information cascades. People on social media observe the choices made by those before them and then react to that. If a video has no views or likes, you're more likely to scroll by, even if it's an excellent video, simply because you see it's not getting much engagement and assume it's bad.

Clearly, attention begets more attention, but all of this is exacerbated by the algorithm, which recommends content by predicting how likely people are to engage with it. If a post is better at capturing and holding an audience in the first few minutes, it'll be pushed to far more people in the next few minutes, kickstarting the positive feedback loop.

The resulting difference is huge, and a very small percentage of social media posts dominate a very large percentage of our attention. Since the posts that work often employ specific tactics, like using certain phrases or keywords, those tactics will be self-perpetuated the same way attention has been. Any distinction between trendbait, clickbait, ragebait, and regular words dissolves into the parade of linguistic tricks that emerge (and occasionally stick around) with each successive internet fad.

At the risk of sounding biased, I believe that influencers aren't solely at fault here. Social media platforms are doing the same thing as creators, but on a macro scale. They're trying to keep your attention through any means possible, directly building this conduit for the most attention-grabbing language to reproduce from creator to consumer. Algorithms are the culprits, influencers are the accomplices, language is the weapon, and you, dear reader, are the victim.

# 4

···········

# Why Everybody Sounds the Same Online

S OCIAL MEDIA CAN make us do funny things. For content
creators especially, the creative pressures of our profession
take this to a whole new level. We know that influencers regularly mold their creative and linguistic decisions around the constraints of the algorithm, but in some cases they also shape their
own identities around the goal of optimized content.

In January 2024, a widely circulated video among the Indian
community on TikTok accused the creator Sara Deshmukh of
"faking" her Indian accent, pointing out that she had previously
spoken in an obviously British accent. In response, Sara (who
was born in India and later moved to the U.K.) made a video
saying that there was nothing "fake" about either accent, but that
she had previously felt a pressure to code-switch online—that
is, to present less like an Indian. Following her video, dozens of
other Indian creators spoke up about how this was a very real
issue facing their community.

Sara, who posts as @iconicakes to a community of more than
three million followers, tells me that her code-switching goes

back to a technique she would use to survive the British school system. In order to make friends, she had to learn to use her British accent as her "outside voice" while keeping her Indian accent as her "inside voice." When she eventually started making video content, she considered that an "outside" context, so naturally she used her British accent.

After a while, Sara began to realize that she was "unintentionally whitewashing" herself and began to feel a growing disquietude about masking who she really was online. To be authentic to her audience, she switched back to using her Indian accent, resulting in the online backlash. Sara was disappointed that much of the vitriol came from fellow Indians and attributes this to internalized racism. "A lot of people from my community saw me as 'aspirational,' but only in my British accent," she says. "And [these] were the same people who found me 'embarrassing' in my Indian one."

Sara has a point. Linguists have done tons of research into what makes certain accents sound more "attractive" than others. What they found is that everything just boils down to our personal prejudices. There's nothing *inherent* in a British accent that makes it sound supposedly better than an Indian accent; rather, that perception is socially conditioned into us from our baked-in associations of Britain having wealth and prestige. This is the same with the American accent, which is widely regarded as a reputable way to speak online because of its global prominence. These perceptions, in Sara's opinion, lead to a "glorification of Western culture" that causes people to "Americanize online spaces," even when that means suppressing their own culture.

Again, she's not wrong. Researchers have been commenting on the "Americanization" of culture ever since Hollywood began dominating the global film industry in the 1910s. Since then, America has only risen as a global power, exporting and imposing its cultural hegemony on other countries around the world.

(Just look at the twenty-three thousand McDonald's restaurants outside the United States.) This effect, however, has been particularly powerful in the online space. American tech behemoths control huge shares of the global market, and American English has become the lingua franca of internet communication. The sheer export of American ideas on these apps has led to a pressure for users to conform to an overwhelmingly U.S.-centric style of communication.

As the largest English-speaking country by far, America also boasts a massive plurality of English-language social media users, who expect content to conform to their cultural expectations. Fully 43 percent of my Instagram Reels viewers are from the United States, which is an enormous difference when compared with the U.K. in second place with 7 percent. The differences are even more stark on YouTube and TikTok. The knowledge gleaned from this data sends me a clear message as a creator: I primarily need to cater to an American audience.

Influencers are constantly pressured by social media to gravitate toward their mean audience, for it both avoids stigmatization and generates the most consistent interaction. This is easy for me as an American, but many international creators feel as if they have to "soften" their accents to sound more American and thus appeal to their target demographic. And of course, every time someone conforms, it becomes more and more expected for others to do the same.

In effect, we've launched an inexorable, performative genericization of the English language, which may even be having real effects on how people speak offline. In 2020, *The Guardian* reported that British children were increasingly speaking in American-sounding "YouTube accents" during the pandemic due to the predominantly American content they consumed online.[1] A similar phenomenon is happening on a worldwide scale. Regional accents have already been disappearing since the onset of globalization, but the internet (and social media in particular) is accelerating that to a greater degree than ever before.

. . . . . . . .

Accents have always been socially conditioned. In the past, those conditions have usually been some combination of who your parents are, who your friends are, and where you live. The internet has become another shaping factor—and a powerful one at that.

In January 2024, NPR reached out to interview me about a new "TikTok accent" that had developed entirely online. The concept first started getting buzz in late 2023, so NPR was surprisingly ahead of the game for a traditional media outlet, but in another sense it was quite late. The accent had already been around in its modern form for at least five years, and until that point very few people had commented on it.

If you consume short-form video content, you're probably familiar with what I'm referring to. Many creators, especially female lifestyle influencers, are seen as speaking with a distinctive inflection pattern. It's mostly audible in tutorial or storytelling content, and also occurs on apps like Instagram and YouTube, which is why I'll be calling it the "influencer accent" instead of the "TikTok accent."

The most noticeable characteristic is uptalk, or a rising intonation at the end of a sentence that makes it sound almost like a question. The placement of the uptalk follows a predictable rhythm in spoken sentences: The final stressed syllable takes on a rising tone and is followed by high tones until the sentence is completed. If we assume a caron ($\check{a}$) to indicate a rising tone and an acute accent ($\acute{a}$) to indicate a high tone, then the sentence "Hey, guys, today we're trying this new makeup brand from Sephora" would sound like this:

Hěy, gúys
today we're trying this new mǎkeúp bránd
from Sephŏrá

In this case, the accents on "makeup brand" are optional. The influencer could instead choose to barrel through the sentence while only uptalking on "Hey, guys" and "Sephora." This would be consistent with other uptalking accents, such as the Valley girl accent from Southern California. However, a common feature of the influencer accent is *emphatic prosody,* or the decision to stress more words than necessary. Instead of the intuitive emphatic patterns you might use, the typical influencer also accents important keywords like "makeup brand." This choice marks a clear departure from the Valley girl voice. By uptalking even when it's not the end of a sentence, the influencers better focus your attention on the content of what they're saying.

I also broke up our example sentence into three parts because I wanted to highlight its cadence. The influencer accent will frequently include lengthy pauses after the rising intonations, and oftentimes the final vowel will be lengthened to drag the word out. In some variations, influencers will also increase the *rhoticity* (pronunciation of the *r* sound) of a word to make that word linger.

Nevertheless, the influencer accent remains unique precisely because it spread in response to social media algorithms. Much like the linguistic microhooks I scatter throughout my videos, the usage of this accent is fundamentally an attempt to maximize viewer retention. The uptalk, for example, serves an important function by making each sentence sound unfinished. You as the viewer feel as if something is coming next, so you keep watching to get the dopamine hit of hearing what it is. At the same time, the rising tone makes it sound almost as though the creator is constantly asking you for your opinion, which keeps you interested and engaged. Uptalk has long been regarded as a sign of uncertainty, and by using it, the influencer gives the illusion of seeking validation from you.

This almost conversational aspect to the influencer accent erodes the boundary between one-sided and two-sided communication, making it easier for you to feel engaged with the creator. Viewers can even start to develop a parasocial connection to the influencer, where they develop feelings of personal intimacy and familiarity with the creator, despite not knowing them in person. This, of course, is great for retention.

In conversation analysis, the offline equivalent of retention is called *floor holding*. Think of how a stand-up comedian needs more than jokes to entertain an audience. They need rhythm, timing, and nonverbal cues to "hold the floor" of the interaction, keeping your attention so they can deliver their jokes. The influencer has a similar but virtual arsenal of tricks that extend well beyond just uptalk.

Emphatic prosody is incredible for floor holding. Our brains like to be completely absorbed in an experience, and the lullaby-esque, lilting tones of the influencer accent scratch that itch while simultaneously enveloping us in a loop of engagement tactics.[2] Now that every other word is emphasized, we're drawn in multiple times in each sentence. If your attention starts drifting, the added stress pulls you right back, making it harder to break away and easier to personally resonate with a video.

Meanwhile, the vowel lengthening and overemphasis of the *r* sound are also textbook retention strategies because they keep us hanging on the elongated word. If you look at a children's show like *Sesame Street*, you'll see the exact same thing happening. The characters will frequently lengthen their vowels, not only to make it easier for kids to understand them, but also to continuously recapture their young audience's attention. *Hi, kiiids! Today we're learning the alphabeeet!* In this era of information overload, influencers are turning to the same floor-holding strategies we use to entertain toddlers.

The lengthened words further serve to cover up any pauses that might follow an influencer's sentence. Obviously, pauses are bad for the algorithm; few things are less interesting to viewers than dead air. Silence breaks the illusion that you're experiencing a fun little world and reminds you that you're just a person staring at a screen. Influencers, especially those working in an extemporaneous or improvisational capacity, therefore need to find a way to avoid silence. That's where the rising tones and longer word sounds come in.

Out of the dozen or so videos I've seen of creators breaking down their accents, several of them noted that they do this intentionally. Influencers need time to think, so they leave us with an auditory breadcrumb while they're stringing together their next thought. The vowels and *r* sounds filling their pauses are actually little reminders indicating that "I'm not done yet; there's actually more to come." You can see how anathema silence is to influencers by how we start our videos. When we record, we *immediately* launch into talking, because even half a second of silence is enough for people to scroll away. I actually intentionally trim the beginnings of my videos to eliminate any gaps, and I know many other creators do the same.

We do this so frequently that it's become a running joke when people *don't* instantly start talking. We call that the *millennial pause,* a pejorative term highlighting how different generations engage with the social media space. You can see it in most videos posted by Taylor Swift, our most famous millennial. She'll always blink for half a second and then start talking. In contrast, any Gen Z creator will already be deep in conversation as soon as the video starts.[3]

There are several proposed theories for this schism: Millennials are less accustomed to social media; millennials are making sure their devices are properly recording; millennials are still used to old video equipment. Some combination of these theories absolutely contributes to why millennials *don't* immediately start talking, but I'm more interested in why younger creators *do*—and we *do* immediately start talking because we've been conditioned to constantly stimulate our viewers. Any little break in their entertainment hurts our chances of virality.

We take this so far that we'll even add an extra opening strategy called the *Gen Z shake*. As soon as a creator starts their video with the phone in their hand, they'll set it down on a surface, causing the viewer's perspective to suddenly shake. This is a very deliberate, planned tactic meant to visually disrupt scrolling patterns and capture attention at the beginning of a video. It's also a semiotic signal foreshadowing an interesting anecdote.

If we're willing to modify our recording strategies for attention, then why not our accents? Just as Sara Deshmukh felt that she would be able to better hold on to her audience with a British accent, many creators feel that they can better hold on to *their* audiences through their "influencer accents."

........

In September 2024, an employee of MrBeast—the world's most successful YouTuber—leaked a thirty-six-page onboarding memo revealing the strategies he uses to consistently go viral. The memo shows that his success is anything but coincidence: Throughout the document, he meticulously breaks down his creative decisions into extremely analytical explanations of how everything is engineered to improve his retention rate.[4]

This invaluable insight into MrBeast's headspace proves that creators at the top level must be deliberate in order to keep succeeding. It's not about quality so much as it is about attention: In his own words, "99% of movies or tv shows would flop on

YouTube" because they're not as good at engaging the audience. He treats YouTube as a unique medium and strongly believes that "the more extreme [a video is] the better."

The memo also perfectly explains his linguistic decisions. If you watch MrBeast's videos, you'll notice that he MAKES EVERY WORD POP FOR MAXIMUM EXCITEMENT! He's constantly stimulating his audience to keep them maximally engaged. I call this the *entertainment influencer accent,* and it's distinctly identifiable from the "lifestyle influencer accent," even though at their core they do the same thing. Both are trying to hold on to their audience, but the entertainment influencer does this through a more extremely enthusiastic style.

MrBeast's earlier videos are a historical treasure trove, revealing just how he modified his accent over time. In the beginning, he spoke in a slower-paced, less compelling way: A lexical analysis published by the YouTube channel Data Time clocked his initial speed at 170 words per minute (wpm), compared with 140 wpm for the average English speaker. Today, he hovers just under 200 wpm, indicating that he sped up his speaking style to help with retention. The evidence gets even more damning if we look at the variance in his talking speed over time. His earliest content has a standard deviation of 42 wpm, while his current videos are down to a deviation of only 14 wpm. Clearly, he initially experimented with different speeds until finally homing in on a specific cadence that works best for him.

If you look at any interview of MrBeast, and then compare that with how he speaks in his YouTube videos, you'll quickly realize that MrBeast doesn't use his influencer accent in real life. Instead, he code-switches in the same way that Sara code-switched into the British accent: He speaks a certain way because he feels that it'll perform better online. The same is true for all his disciples: One German entertainment influencer I surveyed noted that he intentionally increased his pitch, held his breath, and made his words more energetic—all because he knew it helped him build his audience of more than 600,000 followers. This was distinctly different from his natural voice, but it did cause an issue when he started using his "video" voice too frequently in person and had to go to a speech therapist to "fix" it.

Thousands of other influencers are similarly trying to replicate MrBeast's success, a phenomenon that has been described as the *Beastification* of social media. This is happening not only with content style but also with language. In a poll I conducted of forty-five influencers (with follower counts ranging between 10,000 and 3 million), 64 percent agreed that they consciously chose to modify their speech online, with two-thirds of that group directly citing their knowledge of social media metrics as the reason behind that decision.

Whether they're lifestyle influencers or Beastified entertainment influencers, it's very clear that at least some people are intentionally modifying their language to fit the online medium. Many of the creators I spoke to specifically noted that they alter their cadence and sentence stress, providing further evidence that the emphatic prosody trend is deliberate. Over *time,* creators have *figured out* that emphasizing *certain words* helps videos *perform better*.

While some people directly emulate more successful influencers, video analytics are also an incredible tool for figuring out how to speak addictively. If I look at my video performance and see a sudden drop in retention at a particular time interval, I can then check exactly what happened at that time that might have caused me to lose viewers. Over time, I can figure out what my audience does and doesn't want to hear, and piece together the conclusion "Oh, if I stress more words, I'll have better retention." This must have at least played a part in the emphatic prosody boom, because it's certainly why I started talking like that.

Sophia Smith Galer, a journalist with more than half a million followers on TikTok, published an excellent explanation of this in a January 2024 article for *BBC Future*. "We are perhaps linguistically responding to what we think is going to perform well on the algorithm," she wrote, noting that it works best when you "never sound like you're finishing a sentence." Basically, we're behaviorally conditioned through trial and error into talking this way.[5]

Sophia is not a lifestyle creator with a stereotypical "influencer accent," nor is she giving away large sums of money like MrBeast; instead, she makes well-researched, educational content on linguistics as I do. Nevertheless, we both employ noticeably emphatic prosody and uptalk in our videos. Our presentation styles have their own feel. Sophia tells me that she tries to speak "somewhere in between broadcaster and creator" when she makes content, instead of using her usual "news voice."

That's because there are more internet accents than people think. The "lifestyle influencer accent" is simply the most stereotyped iteration since it's highly noticeable and easy to make fun of. Sophia and I have a third speaking style that I call the *educational influencer accent,* which keeps the pitch variation but characteristically includes much faster and more energetic articulation than we use in real life (yet not as over-the-top as an entertainment influencer).

My friends have definitely made fun of me for this. If I get into an excited explanation of something, they'll joke that I'm starting to slip into my "online accent." At this point, though, it comes very naturally. I transition in and out of it without any thought. I uptalk. I stress certain words. I speak faster. While I'm not a beauty influencer by any regard, I've absolutely felt myself become slowly trained into using my own style of "influencer accent," to the point where it's now second nature.

I don't mean to chalk it all up to a Pavlovian response. When I say I was "conditioned," I mean that I was intentionally trying out different ways of speaking until I found the elements that worked best for my content style. I started out speaking normally, unsure of how to talk into a camera. Over time, I sped up my voice and employed different intonation styles that I saw other creators use. Eventually, I settled on the version that performed best overall.

To this day, I re-record certain takes whenever I feel as if I stressed the wrong word or didn't talk fast enough to hold on to my audience. There's certainly some degree of intentionality, but it's the same with any habit-forming process. Eventually, the conscious decisions become routine, then effortless. I really don't think too much about it anymore, and much of my "influencer accent" has now become intuitive. As a bonus, it continues to help other engagement metrics: I often get comments saying either that I talk too fast or that I talk at the perfect speed, so my posts get engagement (and therefore traction) simply because I talk quickly.

········

There's definitely a blurred line between what qualifies as a "conscious" and a "subconscious" influencer accent. Sometimes, like in my case, it starts out as very deliberate, then ends up in a more intuitive code-switching context. In the case of the German influencer, it directly bled into his everyday life. Then there are the 30 percent of content creators who say they've never consciously tried to use an "influencer accent," but ended up with one anyway.

If you're wondering how someone might subconsciously end up with an accent, it's actually not that surprising. Accents are fluid. Someone who moves from Australia to America will likely start to speak more "American" over time, either because they're intentionally trying to assimilate or because they're unintentionally imitating those around them. This happens even more easily when we're code-switching, because there's social value in sounding like each other. We always tend to copy those around us, and many creators may be imitating other creators because that's how they think someone is supposed to speak online.

Once again, American frat bros give us a great analogy. If you visit any U.S. college fraternity, you'll almost definitely find the same "fraccent" being used by frat bros—all the way from California to Massachusetts. Despite coming from different backgrounds, they all suddenly adopt a similar vocal-fried drawl as soon as they start rushing. Many aren't doing it intentionally. They hear others using it, internalize that as how they should be talking, and begin using it themselves as part of their shared sociolect.

Traditionally, the "subconscious" versus "conscious" distinction has been used to differentiate between accents and *affectations,* which are considered "forced" accents, like when Americans pretend to speak British. In truth, that's kind of a stupid distinction, because many acquired accents can start out as "forced." If you keep pretending to speak British, you'll eventually start to actually have a British accent, just like the Australian who becomes more "American" over time. And, as we've seen, it can be more of a gradient than a black-and-white dichotomy. Some frat bros, for example, probably *do* force their accent, which would mean the "fraccent" is simultaneously an accent and an affectation, depending on the speaker.

The fact that the influencer accent *can* have the "subconscious" characteristic of a "naturally acquired" accent means that it can spread by itself, without people even needing to figure out that it's good for the algorithm. Instead of getting overly analytical like myself or MrBeast, some creators may simply start talking that way because they assume it's the natural way to speak on social media (and then the accent self-perpetuates from there).

The implicit assumption that there's a correct way to talk online is the same assumption that the frat bros make when adopting the fraccent. They hear others talking that way and assimilate, because it's more appropriate to that particular social situation. They may feel that there's an expectation to present a certain way, that it could even make them seem cooler, or that it could earn them respect. In linguistics, we call this a *prestige dialect*—an accent associated with a desirable social or economic class. Think of it like a sociolect on steroids.

Prestige dialects are unavoidable, and happen all the time. In the U.K., the Received Pronunciation (also known as the Queen's English) is considered a more prestigious form of speaking, even though there are many valid subdialects of British English. Similarly, the General American English accent is considered more "correct" in America, leading to the discrimination of other dialects like Appalachian English and African American English. We carry these biases over to our consumption of media, which is why we prefer it when creators base their accents on either General American English or the Received Pronunciation.

Because of their perceived social value, prestige dialects are often adopted by people trying to improve their social status. The Australian immigrant would much rather learn General American English than Appalachian English because it's associated with greater wealth and social mobility. Similarly, the "influencer" prestige dialects are tied to the social class of "influencers," who are perceived more positively than "non-influencers" in the online space. When someone is just starting to make content online, they want to be thought of as belonging to the former group, so they may consciously or subconsciously speak that way. That's why we suddenly have so many entertainment influencers talking like MrBeast.

The craziest part is that the fake-it-till-you-make-it strategy actually works on viewers. Once again, it all comes down to framing: Your brain is trained to constantly evaluate situations for how likely they are to benefit you. If you're scrolling on social media and you come across a dimly lit, grainy video, you'll probably scroll away, even if the content would otherwise be extremely interesting or entertaining. Since most high-quality videos use good lighting and camera definition, you're conditioned to respond positively to content with those characteristics.

The same is true for the influencer accent, which triggers a categorization in your mind and frames your perception of how much you think you're going to enjoy the video. By now, someone who enjoys watching makeup tutorials is accustomed to the best tutorials being delivered in the "lifestyle influencer accent." If they see a creator using it, their brain tells them to keep watching for the expected positive experience. Conversely, if a creator starts their tutorial in a monotone deadpan, the viewer's brain will tell them to scroll away, because it doesn't match up with previous rewarding experiences. This makes a huge difference when bad first impressions can cost creators 50 percent of their retention rate in the very first second. We have no option but to prime you with metalinguistic signals like the influencer accent.

It's a funny little tango, isn't it? The influencer is telling you "I'm an influencer, so you should listen to me," while you as the consumer get the message "They're an influencer, so I should listen to them." If you combine that with the other addictive linguistic tricks we've already discussed, you can see why the influencer accent has such a grip on social media.

. . . . . . . .

We're actually quite used to prestige dialects in the media. Think how jarring it would be to hear your Channel 10 anchor speak in a thick Appalachian accent. You expect to get your nightly news in the same bland broadcaster voice you've been hearing your whole life, and this isn't a coincidence. Traditionally, journalists have been trained to eschew their regional accents in favor of a more "neutral" American dialect, which uses the same standard pronunciation and authoritative rhythm that you'll hear on any news segment. And it works. It's established. It commands respect and attention. Meanwhile, other accents might make you more likely to change the channel.

Before the modern era of broadcasting, there was also the *transatlantic accent,* that half-American, half-British dialect you probably associate with fast-talking actors in old-timey black-and-white movies. Until the mid-twentieth century, everybody working in the entertainment industry was expected to be versed in the accent, which served to audibly separate the wealthy upper class from the less educated lower classes.

Both the transatlantic accent and the broadcaster voice are affectations, intentionally taught to create prestigious in-groups and consciously acquired by their speakers. They are highly regarded precisely because of their exclusivity. The influencer accent, however, is much more democratic, since it's entirely self-taught. There's no gatekeeping; everyone has to figure it out themselves.

How, though, can a prestige dialect become so widespread without the deliberate propagation of an elite in-group? There are so many other ways online creators could potentially capture your attention, but we ended up with the identifiable "influencer accents" that we have. Can this really be boiled down to mere social psychology and algorithmic pressures?

We can, in fact, work backward to figure out why this happened. The "lifestyle influencer accent" that's popular on social media today is only the most recent iteration of how beauty vloggers talk online. Before TikTok, the most popular video platform was YouTube, and commenters identified a "YouTube voice" as early as 2015 in an *Atlantic* article, which noted that YouTubers overstress their words, lengthen their vowels, and use a specific cadence to keep the attention of their audience.[6] Sound familiar?

It's not surprising that the TikTok-era influencer accent comes from the YouTube-era influencer accent, because many early video creators on TikTok likely took their cues from creators on the larger platform. For beauty and lifestyle influencers especially, vloggers and fashion creators were built-in resources from whom to learn. But we can go back even further, because even YouTube creators had to take their cues from somewhere.

Part of their accent just came out of the one-sided nature of video communication. Monologues are fundamentally different from conversational speech. They're given with the intention of delivering an uninterrupted message. That's why the uptalk in the influencer accent can be oddly reminiscent of a voicemail on an answering machine, and why the stress patterns *are* kind of similar to those of the broadcaster voice. We talk a certain way when we want to keep attention but we're not expecting a response.

The other source of the lifestyle YouTube accent is a real-life accent that I've already mentioned—the Valley girl accent. Before YouTube got popular, the equivalent of social media influencers were celebrities like Paris Hilton and the Kardashians, who speak with the same kind of uptalk still used by many creators today. Because these figures were the standard of female beauty and fashion at the time, their speaking style was adopted by others trying to present a high-class lifestyle.

Early influences like these are incredibly important, because the first users of a website have a tremendous impact on its linguistic culture. This is called the *linguistic founder effect*. People always look to those before them for social cues. Since the earliest YouTube creators copied the Kardashians and the earliest TikTok creators copied YouTubers, the Kardashian-derivative dialects became established norms on their respective platforms, and were thus seen as prestigious simply because they were the standard ways of speaking. From these bottlenecks, the accents then spread to later users, eventually trickling down to micro-influencers and everyday social media users trying to fit in online.

Michael Stevens, an early educational YouTuber posting as "Vsauce" to an audience of twenty-three million, demonstrates how this process started for the "educational influencer accent." When I spoke to him, he insisted that he had never consciously modified his accent, but that he was instead "unconsciously responding to cues I get from others." Over time, he sped up his talking pace and leaned into a specific persona because "viewers (and algorithms) do come to expect a certain style"—but he did this simply by feeling out what made sense.

Without prompting, Michael then began pointing out how he had observed the linguistic founder effect in the formation of his and later influencers' accents. "I've always felt that most influencer accents and tropes followed from early adopters," he tells me. "They picked up what makes people enjoy watching and listening and then later others coded it and tried to deliberately imitate it."

At the same time, most educational creators today see Michael as a hugely influential early adopter himself. His accent, too, fits into a long, complicated lineage of people copying each other, both subconsciously and consciously, and then selecting for the techniques that work best with their content style and platform.

. . . . . . . .

Whenever people ask me about the "influencer accent," they're usually asking about the "lifestyle influencer accent." In reality, as you now know, there are many distinct creator speaking styles, which is why I've been careful to separate the different types.

The modern-day "lifestyle influencer accent" is probably talked about most because it's used by young women, whose linguistic choices are more frequently scrutinized than those of other linguistic innovators. Even though it's not doing anything different from my "educational influencer accent" or MrBeast's "entertainment influencer accent," it's stereotyped more because society tends to pay more attention to, and criticize, how women talk. Like the stigmatization of the Indian accent over the British accent, our attitudes toward it are entirely culturally constructed.

Despite popular perception, a beauty influencer isn't being any more "phony" than Sara Deshmukh, and neither of them is any more "phony" than myself or MrBeast. We're all code-switching online to best reach our audience. Nobody presents a constant identity in every situation, not even you. You talk differently around different people, depending on the social context and domain of use.

In a way, the various "influencer accents" were inevitable adaptations to the online communicative medium. Of course it was going to be different from in-person conversations, and as such would require a uniquely adapted way of speaking. Remember how MrBeast wrote that "99% of movies . . . would flop on YouTube." That's not because the movies are bad but because YouTube is a different medium targeted toward maximizing attention, and you have to adapt to that medium if you want to be successful.

The breadth of ways people have differentiated their accents poses an interesting contradiction. On the one hand, there is a trend toward online uniformity. We'll definitely be seeing more people adopt the fast-paced, overemphasized American influencer accent, while regional geographic dialects continue to die out.

On the other hand, there's still a lot of diversity on the internet. A beauty influencer speaking off the cuff to her audience will be using a separate set of tools than those I am, since I script out educational videos with a different audience in mind. Lengthened vowels and uptalk might work better for her purpose and delivery style, while a fast-paced energetic delivery might work better for mine. In that sense, even though influencer accents had to go through a bottleneck of algorithmic pressures and preexisting social expectations, they're also branching out in their own unique ways.

This contradiction is a microcosm of social media at large. The algorithm simultaneously unites us and divides us by creating a common online culture and then dividing us into smaller and smaller groups for us to create our own subcultures.

# 5

...........

## "The Algorithm Really Knows Me"

THERE'S NO QUESTION whether social media has homoge-
nized mass culture. Viral trends connect every corner of the
internet, and every creator's content style is unavoidably subordinated to a rigid set of algorithmic pressures.

Paradoxically, however, the very recommendation systems
responsible for imposing broader cultural uniformity have also
brought about a simultaneous renaissance in niche interests.
Yes, social media platforms want to standardize certain aspects
of the online experience, but they're also motivated to personalize it. You engage more when your content is targeted to your
interests, and the more niche communities that exist, the more
content can be targeted toward you.

Remember how social groups can develop their own way of
speaking called a sociolect? That's happening everywhere online
now. In 2023, *Wired* reported on the emergence of a "Swiftie
fanilect"—a distinct sociolect uniquely recognizable among
Taylor Swift fans.[1]

If you're a Taylor fan, or you know a fan, this should make a lot of sense. It really can feel as if her audience were speaking a separate language at times. Phrases like "red scarf" and "invisible string" or the number 13 can mean something completely different to a Swiftie. Collectively, the community has built up its own vocabulary, including an ever-growing list of portmanteaus like "Gaylor" (the fan theory that Taylor is actually gay), "Haylor" (her "couple name" with Harry Styles), and "Hiddleswift" (her couple name with Tom Hiddleston).

This hodgepodge of intertextual references, fan theories, and specialized terminology would not have been nearly as extensive without the presence of social media algorithms. By targeting Taylor-related content specifically to Swifties, platforms like TikTok and Instagram gave them a community in which to gather. Each video, stitch, and comment section became a welcome space to share wild speculations, explain references, and connect with like-minded people.

With community, slang proliferated. Now that Swifties had a place to talk to other Swifties, they also developed a shared need to invent and spread words for topics important to them—whether those topics were ship names or long-shot sapphic analyses. This is how new words are always created. They're never spontaneously adopted by everyone, but rather emerge out of in-groups with common interests and a common incentive to fill the "semantic gaps" in their vocabularies. Beyond their useful meanings, they are also a way to demonstrate and feel belongingness to the greater Swiftie community.

This phenomenon is hardly isolated to Swifties. K-pop fandom has an extensive fanilect built up around their subculture that can sound completely unrecognizable to an average English speaker. Some terms, like the Korean loanwords *aegyo* (the cutest member of a group) and *sasaeng* (an unhealthily obsessed fan), are indecipherable unless you have a specific knowledge of Korean language and culture. Others, like *bias* (one's favorite idol in a group) and *anti* (someone who doesn't like a group), are confusingly repurposed versions of existing words, à la "invisible string" and "red scarf." These expressions make sense to their community, because they are group vocabulary words connecting their shared experience.

The K-pop fanilect is a reflection of and testament to their online connectedness. On TikTok alone, the hashtag #kpop has been used in more than sixty million videos, and there are hundreds of filters to rank who your favorite *bias* is. At the same time, I've never seen a single K-pop video in my entire time on the app.

Nor do I get Taylor Swift content with any regularity. That's because I'm not the intended audience. The highly personalized recommendation systems of modern social media mean that everyone's feed will look very different. While mine is full of people talking about linguistics, the average K-pop stan's will be full of people using words like *anti* and *aegyo*. Meanwhile, I had my friend Ina—the most hard-core Swiftie I know—do a count, and fully four out of every ten videos on their recommended feed were related to Taylor Swift.

The creators of those videos knew that the algorithm would push their content to the right audience, so they felt empowered to geek out by using their fanilect. If anything, the more fanilect-specific words they used, the more metadata the algorithm had, which enabled it to know to whom to send the video. Communities and their languages form simultaneously, which is great for the people in those communities. Ina loves how Taylor's lyrics are just "a part of language now," and delights in how her song titles are commonly used as nouns and adjectives. To Swifties, this is just another way of bonding with others in their in-group.

. . . . . . . . .

Humans have been separating each other into groups as long as we've been around. Neurologists have identified an innate tendency of the human brain to divide the world into "us" and "them," which makes sense from an evolutionary perspective. Belonging to an in-group has historically meant better access to resources, a mutual network of protection, and a social support system. All of these are necessary for survival, and we've brought that into the modern age through concepts such as cliques and countries.

We tend to form these groups with people who are like us. Within the group, there's more of a shared social goal, and thus more to connect over. In sociology, this concept is called *homophily,* literally "loving the same." We identify more strongly with people in the same situation, whether that's socioeconomic status, geographic location, or obsession over a pop star. From these groups, we then build and reinforce our social identities, constructing our concepts of self out of that group membership. If you feel happy being a part of the K-pop fandom group, that affirms your identity as a K-pop fan and strengthens your ties to the group.

One way to build group identity is to gravitate toward the same social behaviors. If you're a K-pop fan, obsession over an idol is just the first step. To reinforce your constructed social identity and signal affinity to others in your group, you might also start dressing in the latest Korean fashion or post about new album releases on social media. These actions tell both yourself and the others in your in-group that you are part of *us,* not *them.*

You'll also use group-specific language. Just like fashion or performative social media posts, language is a form of self-expression used to show a sense of belonging. Again, that's why everybody code-switches: We change how we talk to show we're part of a group. Individual words are tools that can be created or adopted to better bond with each other.

We've already learned how influencers and frat bros use linguistic cues to indicate something important about their identity, but literally everybody does this across multiple domains of use. All families speak in unique *familects*—intimate registers of communication characterized by certain words or expressions only recognizable to that family—and all romantic partners teach each other a secret language that can't be spoken with anyone else.* The same is true for fandom groups. Their in-jokes and references bond them together through shared experience and cultural capital, further differentiating them from the outgroups that aren't caught up or might not even register those phrases in the first place.

Over time, groups perpetuate their own exclusivity as their references become more and more esoteric. It might feel strange to suddenly join a well-established friend group, because you'd have to catch up on all the history. In the same way, it feels strange to me to look into the K-pop or Swiftie fandoms as a relative outsider. On the other hand, if I *had* felt strongly inclined toward these groups, I would have put in the requisite effort to catch myself up on the background knowledge and then joined the group.

In the social media era, the "requisite effort" is just a willingness to watch and engage with in-group content online. The more you interact, the more the algorithm pushes progressively niche content, simultaneously familiarizing you with the group norms and probing your interest in consuming more of the same content. If you scroll away, however, the algorithm will categorize you as part of the out-group and send you fewer of those videos.

In effect, group belongingness has become automated around your receptivity to consuming certain content. Your engagement tells the algorithm whether to let you further into a group or

---

* That might have seemed like a normal sentence to most of the population, but die-hard Taylor Swift fans would recognize it as a reference from her *Folklore* album.

gatekeep access. Since we build identities around group belonging, this means that the algorithm plays an important role in
shaping our perceptions of who we are, mimicking the positive
feedback loop you experience in real-life in-groups.

Given that our brains have always been wired for belonging,
it feels especially good to experience that online. Once you're
deep enough into SwiftTok, you begin to feel special every time
you get a Taylor Swift video, because you derive a sense of connection and inclusion from the perception of being around like-
minded individuals. You giggle over all the lyrical references
and excitedly contribute by commenting your own fan theories.
You're a part of the Swiftie sociolect, and doesn't it feel great to
be a part of something? You might even feel surprised at how
well the algorithm "knows you." In reality, though, the algorithm
helped to create your identity.

. . . . . . . .

There's a fairly widespread perception that a person's recommended page is somehow a reflection of their subconscious. My
friends and I have all made fun of each other for how embarrassing videos might have found their ways onto our For You
pages, drawing on the idea that the very recommendation
reveals something innate in our psyche. In any comments section, you'll frequently see phrases like "I built my own FYP" and
"the algorithm really knows me," further implying that one's feed
is a responsive analogy to one's identity.

Of course, there is some truth to that. I get linguistics videos because I like linguistics, and my friend Ina gets Taylor
Swift videos because they like Taylor Swift. At the same time,
though, we're far more complex than that. We have nuanced
and varied interests, many of which never get reflected in our
recommendation pages. What *actually* happens is that our feeds

recommend the content that is already available, is trending, and most closely matches our predicted taste profiles. Social media platforms want to push us into the few categories they know are likely to hold our attention, which means that certain interests will likely be overrepresented and increasingly appear with the positive feedback loop of in-group engagement. As long as a part of us identifies with those interests, we can be drawn further in. Our past online behavior influences what we'll see online in the future; in this sense, we're really the ones "building" our FYPs ourselves.

This phenomenon is called a *filter bubble,* after a 2011 book of the same name. Once the algorithm starts to "know you" by identifying your interests, it will filter out certain information and prioritize whatever you're most likely to engage with. Eventually, however, you'll find yourself in an *echo chamber*—an environment that only reinforces your existing views.

Filter bubbles and echo chambers are usually viewed negatively for their role in propagating fake news and algorithmic radicalization, but literally any in-group has its own social media filter bubble. K-pop stans are disproportionately prioritized for K-pop content recommendations, meaning that other content is necessarily filtered out. The K-pop user gets sucked deeper into the K-pop echo chamber, creating a sense of belongingness that reinforces their view that they like K-pop and the K-pop side of the algorithm.

Most of the existing discussion on social media and the creation of echo chambers focuses either on the argument that algorithms shape human behavior or on the argument that algorithms reflect innate human behaviors. For example, articles on anti-vaxxer filter bubbles tend to claim either that echo chambers are causing people to distrust vaccines or that the echo chambers gave existing anti-vaxxers a place to gather and voice their beliefs.

Both of these perspectives, however, are too reductive. The question "Do algorithms radicalize people?" is the wrong question; neither humans nor machines are that simple. The Princeton computer science professor Arvind Narayanan instead identifies human-algorithm interactions as a *complex system:* a nonlinear phenomenon that can't be boiled down to an easily explained model. Instead, the results of these interactions are *emergent:* They exist only in the context of the greater system. Rather than *just* pushing K-pop fans into an echo chamber, or *creating* an echo chamber because that's what K-pop fans want, the algorithm has complex, emergent results reflective of how humans and algorithms influence each other.[2]

Since language change is now occurring in the context of the algorithm, we can take Narayanan's description and apply it to all our new linguistic developments:

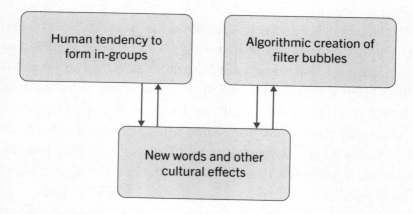

In this graphic, consider the word "Gaylor." The hypothesis that Taylor Swift was secretly weaving lesbian references into her lyrics had been circulating on Tumblr since at least the mid-2010s, with those in the Swiftie in-group excited to bond over their fan theory. For that group, they eventually created the term "Gaylor" to describe their theory. Once the word existed, the

TikTok algorithm was able to use "Gaylor" as a piece of metadata to categorize which videos should be sent to Taylor Swift fans, thus creating a Swiftie echo chamber that was able to further propagate the word in the early 2020s. Not only is the spread of fan vocabulary an emergent effect of human-algorithm interaction, but the very creation of the Taylor Swift filter bubble is an emergent effect of those interactions *plus* the vocabulary. Everything perpetuates itself.

This phenomenon is hardly isolated to echo chambers. If you think back to the previous two chapters, the "influencer accent" and attention-grabbing phrases like "no because" are textbook emergent effects:

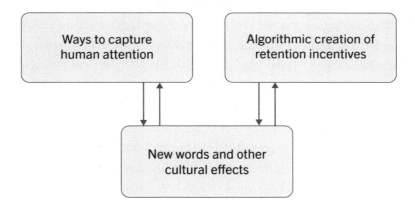

Certain ways of talking are better for capturing attention by virtue of how human attention works. These linguistic techniques are then rewarded by social media platforms, which have a primary goal of profiting off your continued attention. This leads to more creators using those techniques, which helps the words spread. And because we *do* find them captivating on an innate human level, they're then likely to outcompete other bids for your attention, making it that much easier for you to be reeled in.

Now consider chapter 2, which focused on how algorithmic trends help words spread:

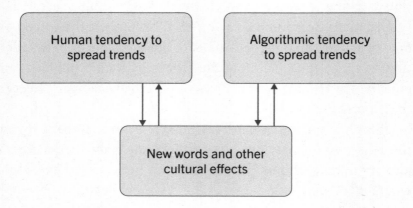

The personalized recommendation algorithm didn't *change* how words spread. Instead, it just added a new factor into the equation. Words have always been tied to fads, reflecting the cultural needs of the day. Sometimes they survive, like the word "O.K." from the Boston newspaper acronym fad. Sometimes they don't, like all the other words from the Boston newspaper acronym fad. That was entirely human behavior at work; fads exist because they hold our interest. They're fun to adopt, and they're great ways to connect to other people.

Online fads, however, are emergent effects of that normal human behavior interacting with the algorithm. Social media platforms want to hold our interest, so they amplify fads. This means that words like "rizz" and "skibidi"—initially spread by humans as fad words—become rewarded metadata that is then spread by the algorithm. This helps them reach popularity faster and to a greater extent than they otherwise might, which in turn influences offline usage.

Finally, let's jump back all the way to the first chapter. The reason I referred to algorithmic censorship as "linguistic Whac-

A-Mole" is that humans are always coming up with new ways to avoid the algorithm, and the algorithm is always trying to respond to new methods of evading censorship.

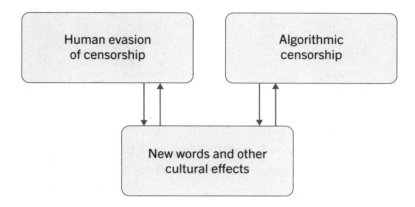

The fact that people are writing out algospeak like "un@l!ve" in their video captions is an emergent effect of the algorithm censoring "kill"; the human creation of the word "unalive"; the subsequent censorship of "unalive"; and the human decision to stylize the writing. Although some kind of death euphemization would still be happening regardless, this particular style and speed of it wouldn't be possible without the game of Whac-A-Mole.

Words can also get entrenched when popularized by new technology. "Hello" wasn't a popular interjection before the advent of the telephone, but simply happened to be a trending fad greeting when phones were being implemented throughout the country. Because it was the right word at the right time, "hello" became standardized as the word to say when answering a call, which is why we still say it today.

In the same way, "unalive" simply happened to be a trending meme right around the time when early TikTok users needed a new way to say "kill." Its adoption was an emergent effect of a human need, an existing trend, and a particular technological moment, but then it got grandfathered into the algospeak sociolect. Today, it's the expected way to speak online, just as "hello" became the expected way to speak on the phone. As we've seen, both words eventually also began to escape those contexts.

········

The unprecedentedly rapid emergence of filter bubbles means that the word formation process is unprecedentedly compounded. Thanks to the internet, people with niche interests can find each other more easily than ever before. In these new bubbles, they create and spread new terms, strengthening their in-group status.

The increasing division of the internet at large is known as "cyberbalkanization," from a 1996 paper describing the early division of online communities into special interest groups. Researchers have written loads of papers connecting this phenomenon to social effects like political polarization, but cyberbalkanization also affects etymology. The more the internet splits into in-group filter bubbles, the more spaces exist for new words to multiply. Most of these words stay in the in-group; that's the point. "Gaylor" and "Hiddleswift" aren't important enough concepts to become mainstream on a large scale, but they are pertinent to the fanilect, where they fill specific semantic gaps for that community.

Occasionally, however, a fanilect word fills a semantic gap for the greater public. After Taylor Swift announced her Eras Tour in late 2022, the phrasal template "in my X era" became a widely popular way to describe a period of one's life. Although some version of the grammatical construction had been circulating in music fandom for a while, it was only truly brought into vogue through the Swiftie fanilect. Since the phrase was easily applicable to a variety of situations, it diffused through memes entirely unrelated to the pop star and was able to leak into general usage among in-person interactions. Like any slang phrase, it caught on as a trend that held our attention.

Around the same time, K-pop culture was making its own impact on mass culture through the word "delulu," which used to exclusively serve as an adjective describing "delusional" fans who believed they would end up in a relationship with their favorite idol. In that sense, the word was too specific to be used by outsiders, but over time the definition broadened to mean "delusional" in general. Suddenly the internet became flooded with memes about people being delulu about their crushes, especially in "manifesting" sentences like "delulu is the solulu" and "delulu is trolulu." Most people didn't even know that the expression came from K-pop stans in the first place.

These words, like their communities, had already been in place for a while, but to a lesser extent. "In my X era" had been a phrasal template since at least the early twenty-first century, and "delulu" had been used by "Koreaboos" on Twitter since at least 2014. However, the terms reached common parlance only in the early 2020s, and that's because the TikTok algorithm gave them a medium to spread. As fans used the phrases in contexts beyond their initial meanings, other people online were able to quickly catch on to that and incorporate that into their own vocabularies.

"Delulu" and "era" followed the same path to widespread usage. First, they were amplified by the emergent in-group/echo chamber system to become popular within a niche community. Then they escaped those communities, becoming broader social media phenomena through the emergent human/algorithm trend system. As more people showed interest in the words, social media platforms kept pushing them to newer audiences, expanding their reach. Since they were catchy and widely applicable, this turned into a positive feedback loop catapulting both terms into mainstream usage.

The underlying process here isn't particularly new: Words have always come from niche communities. In diffusion-of-innovations theory, these communities are the "early adopters" of a word—those who use it before it's widely known. Everyone is an early adopter in some community. You're an early adopter of your familect's unique vocabulary, and if you have any hobbies, you're an early adopter of whatever specialized terminology is used in that hobby. These terms haven't reached the majority yet, but they have the potential to do so if they fill a greater public purpose.

Some niche communities are overrepresented in word dissemination because they bring a lot of new ideas to the masses. For example, the community of tech nerds is responsible for a disproportionately large contribution of computing terms like "software," "hyperlink," and "email." Those words, which used to be niche, are now attached to important concepts that have become adopted by the general public. These words all started in the tech in-group, but then diffused with their associated innovations. Ultimately, they filled a broader societal need for ways to describe these new technologies.

Other groups have less of an impact on mainstream culture, and thus see fewer of their words leave the in-group. The online community of anime fans, for instance, contains many words for describing specific anime tropes, like *yuri, tsundere,* and *yandere.* These terms have very little relevance outside their in-group and are unlikely to spread.

Memes are an exception to this rule. Even if words aren't associated with a practical innovation, they can spread when tied to important cultural concepts. Starting in the early twenty-first century, anime terms like *waifu* (a female character one feels attracted to) and *uwu* (an interjection denoting cuteness) began spreading among younger people as jokes making fun of the anime community. Even though I don't watch anime, I eventually became exposed to these words and then used them ironically with my friends. These words spread between early internet communities because they had cultural capital as memes for people to connect over.

The same thing is happening in the algorithm era. In 2021, the phrase *sussy baka* became a viral meme for describing a "suspicious fool," drawing on the Japanese word for "fool." The expression started out as a self-deprecating joke for members of the anime in-group to make fun of how others in their community talk, but the algorithm quickly figured out that other people also found it funny, so *sussy baka* spread as a humorous expression helping people bond online, ostensibly at the expense of anime fans.

The pattern of *sussy baka* moving from the anime in-group to the general internet in-group follows that of *waifu* or *uwu*, with the key difference being the algorithm. Words aren't just diffusing from human to human anymore: They're now moving from human to algorithm and back to human. *Sussy baka* spread both because it had cultural value and because it was a trending piece of metadata on social media, making the rounds faster than it ever could've before.

Etymology has never been a discipline of pretty stories. Words don't just evolve from point A to point B, but rather develop in the context of greater cultural moments. Language follows human needs, trends, and social groups; all linguistic changes are already emergent effects of a complex system. Technology is yet another complication to that system. We only have the word "O.K." because of human behaviors overlapping with the existence of newspapers; we only have the word "hello" because of human behaviors overlapping with the existence of phones; and we only have *sussy baka* because of human behaviors overlapping with the existence of algorithms.

. . . . . . . .

As a linguist, I'm naturally very excited by all the new words being spread by the algorithm. Each trending term is a riveting opportunity to study the spread of slang, and each filter bubble is a chance to examine how in-groups use sociolects. I also think each linguistic development tells us a story about a wider cultural pattern. Some of the patterns are overwhelmingly positive: It's a good thing that we have new language uniting us, and it's a good thing that people are able to find online communities to develop their shared passions.

However, social media is also a morally gray development, and some words emerging from communities can be repurposed to harm those very communities. While it's probably okay to use *sussy baka* to make fun of anime fans—they're in on the joke and don't face any real hardships—the same isn't true for many marginalized groups.

In early 2023, the word "acoustic" began going viral on TikTok as a humorously pejorative synonym of "autistic." Anytime I posted a video where I seemed passionate about linguistics (so very frequently), I would receive dozens of comments about how I was "definitely acoustic." And it wasn't just me: Many other academic creators would get the same comments, as if all our intellectual curiosities were reducible to autistic hyperfixations.

In this sense, the word "acoustic" started out as an in-joke for the autistic community on TikTok, which had over time built up a safe space in their fairly large filter bubble. Many autistic creators used the word to lightheartedly poke fun at their reality and bond with others in their online community. However, once the word became a meme, it was able to escape the autistic filter bubble to reach the larger TikTok community. Suddenly it was being used by people outside the autistic in-group, and many of these people began using it negatively. Even those who meant it only as an innocent goof inadvertently ended up contributing to the word's pejoration by normalizing the meme's use and perpetuating reductive stereotypes about autism.

This wasn't a one-off occurrence. I watched the same thing happen with the phrases "touch of the tism" and "neurospicy," which similarly spread from the neurodivergent community to take on negative or infantilizing connotations in other corners of social media. This cycle keeps happening because the algorithm creates communities that feel as if they have a space to create and use certain words, but then opens up those same communities just enough to allow certain in-group words to spread with memes and trends.

This is a new phenomenon called *context collapse*. Because there are so many different audiences interacting on social media, communication intended for one audience often finds unintended audiences, which could process it in a different context and then use the information in a new way (in these cases, as general jokes rather than specific in-jokes).[3]

In real life, an in-group can regulate and define linguistic norms fairly well. If you use a word you shouldn't be using, you might be ostracized or reprimanded. These negative social outcomes slow down the word's pejoration. Online, however, groups like the autistic community are unable to police their own vocabulary, and the people taking that vocabulary out of the original community are unable to pick up on how it might not have been for them. Creators speak as if they were talking to their niche, because that's the audience they expect to reach. But, as we've learned, the actual audience is out of their control. In-group language might reach people who don't know they're in the out-group, speeding up the euphemism treadmill.

The edges of a filter bubble aren't very neatly defined. The algorithm might push Taylor Swift videos to my friend Ina 40 percent of the time, but only 10 percent of the time to a less involved fan. There's a gradient of core Swifties to casual Swifties. The more the algorithm thinks a meme has potential outside a core group, the further it pushes it to an outer group, and the same is true for autism videos.

This can pose a big problem, since it's difficult to define who's in the autism in-group beyond social media. Are people who are neurodivergent in some other way justified in using the word "acoustic"? What about people with close autistic friends and relatives? The boundaries are fuzzy, which means the meme invariably gets used by those increasingly peripheral to the original community. This makes it more acceptable for others to replicate their behavior, even those solidly outside the original in-group. Although this is how words diffuse offline, the algorithm tends to erode boundaries faster online. As the in-group words travel more and more to the edges of their original filter bubbles, they are more frequently recommended to those in the out-group, thus enabling their spread and making them lose their original importance inside the in-group.

Autism is an especially useful example for demonstrating this because of the way that social media platforms perpetuate autism misinformation. A 2023 report published by the National Council on Severe Autism highlighted TikTok's unique ability to spread reductive or inaccurate self-diagnosis information through algorithmic recommendations.[4] One video with more than a million views claims that "stirring your ice cream into a creamy texture" is a sign of autism, and thousands of similar videos urge people to self-diagnose themselves with autism spectrum disorder. While there is nothing wrong with self-diagnosis, many people who do self-diagnose on TikTok do so through incorrect or simplistic information on what autism actually is.

This leads to more people feeling adjacent to the in-group and gives in-group words more opportunities to spread. Meanwhile, people with severe autism end up suffering the consequences of in-group words like "acoustic" and "neurospicy" suddenly being repurposed to insult them.

The very nature of modern recommendation algorithms invigorates the spread of misinformation by rewarding outrageous content. A 2019 Facebook memo revealed that its most viral posts had a far greater likelihood of containing misinformation than other posts, because content that sparks division gains more attention and is then pushed by the algorithm.[5] All modern social media platforms work the same way. Even comments trying to correct the misinformation ironically help bolster it, for they also count toward engagement metrics. Because of this, detrimental videos like the ice cream TikTok perform well, furthering false ideas about what qualifies as autism. Now people who may not be autistic feel qualified to use in-group language, applying words like "acoustic" to other situations that don't necessarily indicate autism and inadvertently feeding into the cycle.

. . . . . . . .

Algorithms *themselves* aren't the problem so much as the specific *type* of algorithm being used by the major social media platforms. In his essay on emergent human-algorithm effects, Professor Narayanan points out that the changes we're observing are primarily the result of *engagement optimization* algorithms: recommendation systems built to maximize user interaction. After all, an "algorithm" is just a set of rules optimizing for specific metrics. Social media platforms have chosen to make those metrics targeted around *engagement*: comments, shares, likes, and retention.

While engagement optimization algorithms are good for keeping people in-app, and they genuinely can make the social media experience more entertaining, they're directly responsible for everything you've been learning about in the last four chapters. They reward videos that are good at capturing our attention, and therefore encourage attention-grabbing tactics. They create community filter bubbles for us to connect with, perpetuating in-group language creation. They push memes we'll probably find funny, driving rapid etymological trend cycles.

In a call, Professor Narayanan points out to me that engagement can make or break a word's success. The only content that performs well is typically entertainment oriented, such that words that are "not compatible with fun and those types of content are not going to do as well." Meanwhile, other words that are considered "fun," like trending slang, make it "more fun for people to comment on the video." I've seen this firsthand on videos where I talk about the etymology of trending memes. People like it when I academically dissect a goofy word, and often play into the joke by using that word in the comments. In a TikTok I made on the "in my *X* era" template, for example, I had dozens of comments saying that I was "in my etymology era."

Comments are especially important because they're probably the most heavily weighted engagement metric per view. A comment is worth more than a like because it shows a deeper level of engagement with my content, so I know I want to make videos that goad comments. Often, I know that talking about trending words will do the trick.

Importantly, *engagement* doesn't mean "good." We very often engage with things that are bad for us but nevertheless reel us in. That's why ragebait and misinformation are thriving in the algorithmic era. Professor Narayanan calls this "digital rubbernecking"; people are drawn to react to things they don't like, just as we might be drawn to look at a traffic accident we don't really want to see. In response to this phenomenon, influencers create negative or annoying content to provoke engagement, even to the detriment of the platform as a whole. Since the algorithm optimizes for engagement, we've gotten even more of this negative content as an emergent effect.

Entire communities have been built around digital rubbernecking. After the Rizzler song went viral, a subset of "cringe creators" emerged on TikTok, making videos with embarrassing meme words like "gyat" and "skibidi." By talking in an exaggeratedly degrading manner, they attracted attention from viewers drawn in through secondhand humiliation. In the process, the words "gyat" and "skibidi" continued to spread and dominate our zeitgeist. And while that's a relatively harmless example, the same effect can be true for more dangerous content, which can still be favorably ranked for its ability to capture attention. For example, a 2022 study showed that politicians are engaging in greater online incivility than before because civil content garners less engagement.[6] That's a fairly worrisome development in our already polarized political climate.

In economics and data science, there's an adage called *Goodhart's law,* which warns that "as soon as a metric becomes a target, it ceases to be a good metric." By optimizing for engagement to keep viewers online, social media platforms turned engagement into a target, eventually resulting in engagement-maximizing content that nobody actually wanted.

This is reflected in our attitudes. Research indicates that there's a growing disconnect between what people *want* to see on their recommended feeds and what's *actually* shown on their recommended feeds. The algorithm doesn't reward content in line with what we would consciously choose to see—our *stated* preferences—but instead pushes content aligning with our unconscious, automatic, emotional reactions: our *revealed* preferences. Since your emotions are trained to respond to negative content, you perpetuate negative behavior online, even if you actually only want to see videos of fluffy frolicking kittens.

In response, people are beginning to consciously "train" their algorithms to get more in line with their stated preferences. For example, whenever I get a jazz or classical music video on my recommended feed, I often feel the urge to scroll away because it's not as good at immediately capturing my attention in the highly stimulating online space. However, I know I enjoy jazz and classical music, and I know it's good for me, so I've trained myself to set the phone down and enjoy the song in those moments. The goal is partially to enjoy the video, and partially to tell my algorithm to send me more like it—bringing my stated preferences closer in line with my revealed preferences. My personal identity *isn't* the same thing as my algorithmic identity, but the two are constantly shaping each other on both an active and a passive level.

........

It's hard to avoid engagement optimization in this day and age. Now that every platform is following in TikTok's footsteps, there's very little incentive to change. Engagement earns social media companies more money, and the landscape is far too competitive to shift to more ethically responsible post-ranking systems. Engineers also have surprisingly little control.* Once a machine learning algorithm is programmed a certain way, it becomes impossible to understand why it's doing what it's doing. There's always too much randomness and unpredictability in the complex system to keep track of.

The predominant Silicon Valley ethos stresses neutrality. Software developers are told to exert as little control as possible and

---

* Or understanding of what's happening: algorithms are colloquially called "black boxes" because not even its designers know what's happening under the hood.

adhere to the attitude that "the algorithm knows best." Regardless of whether that's true, the Telecommunications Act of 1996 conveniently absolves online services of any liability for algorithmic recommendations.

Despite their lack of oversight, engagement optimization algorithms have very real effects on our everyday life. For better or worse, they confirm our subconsciously revealed preferences until they become reality, pushing us further into our echo chambers.

Ironically, social media is also an echo chamber that reflects these linguistic patterns on a broader scale. Just as engagement optimization algorithms create linguistically unique in-groups, social media itself is an in-group with its own way of speaking.

Once the phrasal template "in my X era" spread beyond the Swiftie community, it became an example of "TikTok speak," signaling belongingness to the social media in-group. To use it was to show that you were caught up with online culture, confirming your status as part of a much larger echo chamber. Each additional video normalized the phrase for its audience.

Algorithms push trends outside filter bubbles when they have potential to build community across their user base. People like fads because they feel cool; they're seen as exciting social customs within the in-group of popular culture. When a platform like TikTok is the source of these trends, it creates a sense of cutting-edge exclusivity in the greater TikTok-speak filter bubble that everyone wants to be a part of.

But because the boundaries of filter bubbles are fuzzy, words and trends eventually leak out of social media echo chambers to other platforms and then the English language at large. This isn't surprising when you consider that every social media platform steals trending content from other social media platforms. Instagram Reels is full of recycled TikTok videos, TikTok is full of edited YouTube clips, and YouTube is full of material from both websites. Each app has its own culture and language style, but they all exist in a complex ecosystem where they feed into each other. If a trend performs particularly well on one of the platforms, it'll spread beyond it to the others.

Eventually, "in my X era" left the TikTok in-group for the broader internet in-group, which helped the term spread offline. This was no longer just the work of an algorithm anymore; it was a normal human behavior—the same behavior being amplified by the algorithm.

Just as people simultaneously unite over shared ideas and divide over different perspectives, algorithms simultaneously homogenize and diversify us depending on the needs of the tech company. If it's something that helps drive engagement across the platform, like an attentional tactic or widely relatable trend, it will be pushed to everyone. If it's something that helps personalize the experience for you, it will be pushed to the niche community that you're a part of.

Language plays a circular role in identity formation. If you choose to use a certain word, you are accepting that you belong to the group using that word. In the social media era, the algorithm will recognize that, push you deeper into that group, and give you access to more niche language.

The algorithm never *really* "knows" you. It gives you content it thinks you'll engage with, which doesn't initially reflect your identity. Once you consume that content, though, it can and will subtly change you. You may connect more with the niche community in your filter bubble, find that you like certain memes, or start using certain catchy words.

Identity is inherently built as you experience things and form opinions about them. As the algorithm gives you content to experience, you do end up building part of your identity around that, which makes it easier to recommend content to you. In this sense, the algorithm *does* start learning about you. You give it pieces of yourself, and in doing so enter a relationship, continuously renegotiating between the algorithm and your revealed preferences to help construct your identity. Rather than *knowing* you, then, the algorithm moreso *guides* you into who you will become.

# 6

...........

## Wordpilled Slangmaxxing

I ENCOUNTERED MY FIRST INCEL in my junior year of high school. As someone who was chronically on Reddit and highly focused on college applications, I inevitably ended up frequenting the r/ApplyingToCollege subreddit group chat, an enormously helpful resource and supportive community—save for the few self-identified "involuntary celibates" who occasionally showed up to troll the chat.

Whenever the group discussion would stray from college admissions to something like personal relationships, the incels would pop in to proselytize their weirdly detailed philosophy of how our dating prospects are predetermined because of *lookism*—discrimination based on people's looks. In their worldview, the sexual hierarchy was dominated by an elite group of *Chads* (highly attractive men), who could rely on their good looks as a form of "sexual market value" to seduce women at the expense of *betas* (average men who exchange loyalty to Chads for their romantic leftovers). At the very bottom rung were the *incels,* who believed they were unable to have sex because of their appearance.

Acceptance of the lookism philosophy—known as *getting blackpilled*—meant adopting very specific slang and ideas. For example, a Chad was understood to always "mog" (dominate) and "cuck" (emasculate) a beta, but the beta could attempt to improve their status through "looksmaxxing" (enhancing their physical appearance). This might take the form of working out (gymmaxxing) or even seeking physical modifications through "surgerymaxxing."

While most of my Reddit group chat found the incels to be initially entertaining, it soon became pretty clear that their philosophy was actively dangerous. Much of their rhetoric bitterly advocated for violence against women (often dismissed as "foids," "roasties," or "dumpsters") and occurred in the context of actual incel terror attacks that had killed dozens of people. Beyond that, it was just a nuisance for our chat—the incels eventually brought in other incels to disrupt the conversation—so we ended up creating a separate Discord server to freely discuss college and our personal lives without the weird interruptions.

Nevertheless, the entire concept seemed so ridiculous that it was impossible not to poke fun at it. Over the next four years, our newly incel-free group chat continued to ironically use their slang as a shared in-joke. When someone had a project due, for instance, we would say that they were "studypilled" or "homeworkmaxxing." Although these terms were formed through analogy with the incel words "blackpilled" and "looksmaxxing," they were understood to be humorous recombinations and nothing more. It was a stupid, silly shared reference that I never thought would see the light of day beyond our group chat.

You can imagine my surprise, then, when in January 2024 I got a TikTok meme complaining that "it's so hard being a walkpilled cardiomaxxer in a carcel gascucked state like Arizona." I was utterly bemused. Had my recommended feed gotten so targeted that it somehow knew to combine my interest in urban design with my unusually specific knowledge of incel vocabulary?

Within a few weeks, however, I realized that this wasn't just an algorithmic quirk, but rather a genuine phenomenon taking root across social media. People all over the internet were beginning to ironically use incel slang in the same way that my group chat had been doing for years. Creators would make satirical "brainrot videos" about going to "Mogwarts" or engaging in looksmaxxing techniques like *mewing* (a dubious jaw exercise meant to improve facial bone structure).

Perhaps the most shocking thing about the trend was how rapidly it reached mainstream popularity. During a March 2024 lecture at Georgetown University, I had the opportunity to poll my audience: By that point, about 40 percent of the students were familiar with the words. When I repeated the same experiment at Stanford two months later, fully 80 percent had encountered incel vocabulary. Another four months later at Oberlin, and my entire audience recognized the terminology.

The algorithm spread these words by blowing them up as memes. Some of the more general jokes, like mewing, were pushed to, and therefore seen by, everyone. Other jokes were contained to specific filter bubbles. I only got the "walkpilled cardiomaxxer" meme because I was heavily on the urban design side of TikTok, and I love consuming content about architecture and transit. Because of how algorithms recommend similar content in filter bubbles, though, I eventually got more urban design incel videos, like one about being "fossil fuel pilled and bad to the bone" and another about being a "parking lot pilled pavement princess." In the same way, incel memes were able to creep into many other social media in-groups. They were funny and versatile enough to be applied to any concept, from homework to public transit.

I didn't know it during my initial Reddit encounter, but the ideas in that first group chat had spread from an extremist filter bubble to a new, college-related filter bubble. Because of how memes diffuse on the internet, and because of a narrow boundary between irony and authenticity, a potentially dangerous philosophy was beginning to creep through to the general public—bringing its language along with it.

· · · · · · · ·

The modern-day incel is entirely an invention of the twenty-first century. Before the internet, lonely men simply didn't have a way to gather and share ideas. That all began to change in 1997, when a Canadian student started a website called Alana's Involuntary Celibacy Project to connect with others over her shared lack of sex. As the name implies, the site wasn't a place for just straight men; rather, it was used by people of any gender or sexual orientation.

In the early twenty-first century, that initial "incel" community then dispersed to several other websites. These were more male dominated and less moderated, meaning that increasingly misogynistic discussion was able to take root. The largest of these forums, 4chan, doubled as a gathering place for right-wing extremists, whose ideas began to fuse with those of the incels. This is when the modern blackpill philosophy began in earnest.

Notably, 4chan didn't have any user accounts. Every poster was anonymous, meaning that the only way to differentiate yourself as an experienced user was to demonstrate a performative proficiency in shared slang. This unique pressure to show a sense of in-group belonging ended up giving us numerous foundational internet words, such as "troll," "dank," "shitpost," and "rickroll." Using these words was an important way to show that you weren't a "normie" on the website. Because they had wide applicability, they eventually spread beyond the site.

In the same way, most of the highly specific incel vocabulary was built up by 4chan extremists to match their burgeoning ideology. Words like "mogging," "cucked," and "maxxing" became metalinguistic indicators that the anonymous poster was truly a blackpilled member of the community and not some random outsider. You needed to demonstrate a certain level of prerequisite knowledge to truly fit in.

Beyond the technological catalyst of 4chan's user interface, incels have long faced a self-imposed social need to adopt new slang to prove their status. Those within the community fight a constant battle to prove their "purity" as incels and avoid being labeled as "fakecels" or "volcels" (voluntary celibates). Even within the deepest echelons of the incel filter bubble, many believe that most of their peers still have potential to "ascend" to beta status through looksmaxxing, moving location, or accumulating wealth. Only the bottom 1 percent of the population are *truecels*—incels with unchangeably unattractive features and no hope of ascension. In the online space, these truecels are able to dominate the discussion due to their purer status.

Within the incel community itself, language serves the same function as language in a cult: It's a recruitment tool creating an "us versus them" mentality. Since incel vocabulary is used to mark "correct" blackpill philosophy, the incel feels alienated from *normies*—family and friends who don't use the language. Meanwhile, truecel rhetoric pushes recruits to accept more extremist beliefs, since those ideas are associated with higher social status within the community. Those who use the language sound experienced, appearing to understand the ideology well. I personally watched this happen in my original Reddit chat:

Before we split off, the incels managed to convert one of the chat regulars to accept lookism. Before we knew it, he was also spouting propaganda about betas and looksmaxxing.

Through mutual acquaintances, I got in touch with Sofia Correa, a recent University of Florida graduate who anonymously ran one of the largest incel Discord servers in the world. She calls my cult analogy "spot on." What started out as her attempt to troll incel communities turned into a genuine fascination with their language. "It feels exclusive and exciting" to use incel terms, she tells me, especially for people who "were struggling to find a way to make themselves feel better about these faults." Joining the select in-group validates their experiences and gives them a sense of purpose. In a perverse inversion of their initial goals, the degree of "purity" translated to higher "truecel" status. People would proudly use labels like "KHHV" (short for "kissless, hugless, and handholdless virgin") to display their deeper connection to blackpill philosophy, just as a cult has layers of exclusivity to further draw in the acolyte.

The reductive nature of incel language further casts every interaction within their sociological framework. Any dynamic between two men is written off as hierarchical (even though the concepts of "alpha" and "beta" humans have repeatedly been discredited as pseudoscience), and any interaction between men and women is thought of as inherently sexual. Now that the incel is trained to see society in terms of Chads mogging betas, their worldview is limited in a way that ultimately reinforces their ideology; if the only tool you have is a hammer, you tend to see every problem as a nail. Even though Sofia was clearly not an incel, for example, she "couldn't help thinking this way" when she was constantly exposed to the language. Because the ideas were so catchy, she would go through her day "thinking about how other people were mogging" her. Imagine how indoctrinating this mindset can get for someone who truly believes in these terms.

Sofia also notes the perceptually limiting use of *thought-terminating clichés*: loaded expressions that cut off any dissonant thinking. If an incel mentioned a negative experience with a woman, he would be flooded with comments about how "it's over" or "AWALT" (meaning "all women are like that"), which immediately stops any introspection of whether the interaction had some other explanation beyond just lookism. Conversely, if someone had an encouraging or positive experience with a woman, that would be either called a "cope" (implying that it was all in his head) or dismissed as not a "truecel" experience.

In a 2022 paper, the Canadian sociologist Michael Halpin argues that incels intentionally establish their "subordinate masculine status" as a justification for their misogynistic views. By using their truecel purity to legitimize the blackpill philosophy, incels are able to argue against women's agency by advocating for male supremacy, rape, and "sexual redistribution" policies allocating at least one woman to every man.[1] To the incel, these options are more humane than his own existence: The Incels Wiki page explicitly argues that "involuntary celibacy is more painful for men than rape is for women."[2]

Meanwhile, words like "foid" (a portmanteau of "female android") and "dumpster" serve to depersonalize and objectify women, making it easier to remove their agency. Relationships are reduced to purely logical evolutionary processes, allowing the insertion of pseudoscientific terminology and dismissing more nuanced, emotional views of attraction. Sofia tells me that once the incels found out she was a woman, their ideology "made it very hard for them to talk to" her like a human being. Her presence made it difficult for them to reconcile the reality of an actual woman with their idea of what a woman was like. In the end, the latter won out, and Sofia had to abandon her server due to rape and death threats.

. . . . . . . .

If you're wondering why I just told you more about incels than you could ever possibly want to know, I promise there's a point. Incels might be an extreme example, but the basic structure of the incel filter bubble mirrors all other filter bubbles online. Those who are further in the in-group are more likely to dominate discourse, creating and spreading words for those on the periphery. As users familiarize themselves with the group vocabulary, they identify more with that group, and more readily adopt language to fit shared social needs.

I would argue that, if anything, the incel example is very important to understand, for it has probably contributed more to the development of "modern slang" than any other online community. It's precisely *because* of their radicalized and insular echo chamber that they've created so much language and have many more avenues to influence the mainstream. It is *because* of their extreme views that their ideas are so easily spread through memes.

We can, in fact, use the spread of incel ideas as a case study to examine how memes carry information across social media platforms. Real incels never had access to algorithmic recommendations, since their ideology was too extreme. So how did their concepts and language move from website to website until eventually arriving, in diluted form, on our social media feeds?

Let's start where the philosophy began in earnest: 4chan. Despite the forum's early importance, it remained a place where incels mixed with normies. The Incels Wiki page for /r9k/, their main discussion board on 4chan, calls it a "pseudo-incelospherian" space: Although it was a medium "for some genuine incel discussion," it was never purely an incel forum, and "also served as a place for people to pretend to be incel" and troll actual truecels.[3]

Seeking a more insular and supportive community in the mid-2010s, the incel subculture largely turned to Reddit, where subreddits like r/Incels were able to accrue tens of thousands of blackpilled followers. From there, they slowly began pushing their philosophy in other subreddits, which is how I encountered them in my college application group. Forums like these were evidently fruitful recruiting grounds, but the incels found their greatest success on "rate me" subreddits, where people would post pictures of themselves and ask for feedback. Here, incels were able to promote a more accessible version of their philosophy by disguising looksmaxxing language as helpful suggestions. Posters were evaluated on pseudoscientific lookism beauty standards like "interocular distance," "canthal tilt," and "hunter eyes." They were encouraged to improve their facial structure through "mewing" and jaw surgery so that they could "mog" others. If they were interested in exploring further, the blackpill was waiting around the corner.

Even once the incel subreddits were eventually shut down by Reddit, forums like r/RateMe continued to normalize incel jargon, making it easier to both put stock in it and parody it. In the same way that my Discord server jokingly used incel language, jokes about mogging and canthal tilts began to show up in 2021 across Instagram and Twitter, in memes that eventually became viral through TikTok and Instagram Reels.

Ironically, the first people to bring looksmaxxing to TikTok appear to have been women, who unknowingly began repurposing incel concepts from the early "rate me" subreddits. Beauty influencers on #GirlTok would demonstrate how to use canthal tilt to put on eyeliner, or post video filters rating themselves on metrics like forehead size and interocular distance.* Eventually, people began picking up on the phrenological absurdity of these ideas and turned them into more memes. The deeper people poked into the underlying philosophy, the more the jokes multiplied, and words like "pilled" and "-maxxing" were fully trending by late 2023. Most people thought that the concepts were funny and went on to spread them; those who knew the story and were offended by it also helped the terms spread through the ragebait cycle of attention.

Now that we've reached the point where algorithms are involved, the pattern should look fairly familiar. Once the incel terms initially captured our curiosity, they were amplified by the Matthew effect and the engagement treadmill to reach mainstream popularity. Part of their strength rested on how easily they could be recombined into other phrasal templates; part of it rested on their memetic value as catchy comedic references.

As the words took off, they spawned their own spin-off memes. Starting in 2021, for example, the term "sigma" began going viral as an ironic reference to the incel hierarchy of alphas and betas. In this particular joke, a sigma was nominally equal to a Chad, but opted to live outside the normal social structure of their own volition. The phrase started out as a genuinely idolized position within the incelosphere, but was then blown up through memes like the Rizzler song, which contained the lyric "I just wanna be your sigma." A lot of subsequent "brainrot" content focused on similar incel classifications, like an analysis of the power dynamics between dancers in a "TikTok Rizz Party" or viral "sigma face tutorials."

By this point, the words were out of the incels' hands. The community never had the opportunity to gather on major social

---

* Note that each of these terms conveniently worked as viral trendbait terms.

media apps once their subreddits were shut down, and instead had moved to Discord servers like Sofia's or more specific, hard-to-find forums online.

There *have* been past problems with algorithmic filter bubbles leading to extremism: ISIS infamously used YouTube as a recruitment tool in the early 2010s, and the QAnon movement spread in part thanks to Facebook echo chambers. Thankfully, the big platforms had cracked down on more obvious threats by the time incel slang became mainstream. If you look up "incel" on TikTok, for example, it redirects you to a page warning you that your search term is associated with hateful content.

Nevertheless, it's fascinating how far incel humor has reached. One of the most common meme templates on the internet is a crudely drawn comparison of a "Chad walk versus virgin stride." In the original version, the characters are labeled like diagrams in a biology textbook, with annotations pointing out why the Chad's behavior mogs the virgin.

Another widely shared format contrasts the opinion of a crying loser character with that of a confident Chad. Both templates perpetuate incel ideas about social hierarchies, but to the uninitiated they're simply funny conduits for categorizing ideas. These memes—and many others, from "Pepe the Frog" to the "Gigachad"—started on incel-associated 4chan boards before reaching greater popularity on other websites for their easy applicability to everyday situations.

........

By now, we know that the dissemination of incel memes across platforms points to how fringe ideas can become mainstream, and that algorithms can perpetuate dangerous concepts in the name of engagement optimization. The lookism concepts from r/RateMe, including jawline angle, eye distance, and facial symmetry, are eugenics-based talking points that were already regarded as pseudoscientific by the nineteenth century. Now, with beauty influencers making content about those metrics, it feels as if we've reverted to social Darwinist ideas about skull measurement.

Phrenological theories barely scratch the surface of how incel memes open the door to eugenics. Since much of the early incel community was heavily influenced by the alt-right community on 4chan, they've adopted a lot of extreme ideas about interracial relationships. According to lookism philosophy, Asian men are considered the least sexually desirable, and many "truecels" self-identify as "ricecels" or "currycels" as reasons for their inceldom. These men point to WMAF (white male/Asian female) relationships as a principal cause of their virginity—objectifying the women in these situations and depriving them of their agency to make their own dating decisions.

In mid-2024, these ideas somehow also became mainstream through the "Oxford study" meme, which referenced a fictional academic paper on WMAF relationships. Anytime Asian women would post videos featuring white men, they would inevitably get harassed by unsolicited comments calling them an example of the "Oxford study," fetishizing and harassing them over their sexual preferences. A June 2024 article in *The Guardian* identifies this misogynistic scrutiny as mainly stemming from men's rights trolls before it became a widespread meme. The men likely would not have said this to someone's face, but they felt emboldened to comment negatively because of the *online disinhibition effect,* a phenomenon where anonymity makes it easier to spread negativity.[4]

Incel slang is marked by its deeply negative views toward society, and these ideas frequently resonate with younger generations who are similarly pessimistic about the present. In the early 2020s, for instance, the catchphrase "it's over" began making the rounds as a dejected reaction to an adverse situation. Partially a joke, partially a genuine expression of hopelessness, it was buoyed in popularity by incels, who had been using the phrase since it began making the rounds on 4chan.

In her 2024 book, *The Age of Magical Overthinking*, Amanda Montell identifies the rise of "doomslang"—dystopian or detached jargon mostly used by younger people. Hyperbolically negative phrases like "everything sucks" and "I want to kill myself" have become shockingly commonplace, and everyday actions like lying in bed on your phone are bleakly described as "dissociating," "doomscrolling," or "bedrotting." This kind of language is especially common among incels, who were using phrases like "LDAR" ("lay down and rot") before "bedrotting" ever became a thing. The modern doomslang phenomenon appears to have evolved simultaneously with incel-speak, in some cases even being influenced by the latter.

One of the stock characters in the Chad memes, known as the *doomer*, emerged as a way to voice the (frequently incel) dissociated perspective on 4chan, and eventually spread beyond those origins like all the other 4chan memes. Today, I regularly hear my friends calling each other "doomers," as well as using other depressive incel words like "cope," "ropemaxx" (an algospeak replacement for "commit suicide"), and "wagecuck" (someone who works a mindless nine-to-five job). Meanwhile, the term "brainrot," now used to describe a genre of Gen Alpha humor, likely also came from incel circles, which used the expression to describe the perceived decline in intelligence resulting from their lack of social interaction.

These terms spread partially because the algorithm thrives on negativity and partially because they confirmed our existing cultural outlooks. Phrases like "doomer" and "it's over" spoke to our disconnected reality, while "brainrot" held a mirror up to our online addictions and "wagecuck" reflected our growing disenchantment with the American dream. And since apocalyptic statements are good for engagement, the phrases eventually became a part of the zeitgeist, emergently reinforcing our pessimistic points of view. Words are memes, and memes are trends, but all are also *ideas*.

While it's difficult to determine for certain the actual impact of incel vocabulary on our culture, the incels themselves certainly believe they've effectively spread their ideas. On incel sites, longtime truecels use the terms "Newgen" and "Tiktokcel" to describe those who only recently joined their forums from short-form video platforms. The Incels Wiki lists the looksmaxxing trend on TikTok as a primary driver of this recent incel influx, meaning that the meme pipeline has had at least some efficacy in making the blackpill more accessible.

........

If incel memes are so dangerous, how were they able to spread so easily? It all comes down to the very blurred line between comedy and authenticity. To most of us, these memes were just *funny*. We weren't blackpilled by incel language, and we didn't perpetuate them to promote lookism or racism or sexism. Instead, we used them as a form of dark humor, flipping the script on the incel community to ultimately satirize them. When we repurposed the "Chad versus virgin" meme template, the incels became the butt of the joke. When my friends and I used words like "-maxxing" and "pilled," we established a new in-group: the community of young people on social media. The terms were silly jokes to connect over, signaling that we knew something exclusive about popular culture. Since everybody wanted to feel like part of the in-group, the words spread, taking them out of the incels' hands and robbing them of their original power as they simply became "brainrot" words.

I suspect that the vast majority of people sharing the memes probably didn't even know they came from incels. The most disturbing concepts—like calling women "foids" or Asian people "currycels"—remained in-group, because these are far too offensive to become mainstream. But for other concepts such as mewing, there was simply no reason to assume the underlying idea would be problematic until you really looked into it.

Some time after the serious philosophy was turned into a joke, though, it began to be treated seriously again by some of those out of the loop. At least some of the beauty influencers talking about hunter eyes and interocular distance misinterpreted the ironic context of the lookism words and spread them as genuine beauty standards, which spawned more jokes, leading to more serious reinterpretations. After the jokes about canthal tilts and mewing went viral, we began seeing increases in canthal tilt eyeliner demonstrations and Google searches for "jaw surgery." On the one hand, that just made the jokes funnier; on the other, incel ideas about attractiveness became more culturally relevant.

Again, how did this happen? Well, it's famously difficult to discern tone on the internet, to the point where there's an adage about it called *Poe's law:* "Any sarcastic expression of extreme views can be mistaken for a sincere expression of those views," and vice versa.

Poe's law explains how dangerous ideas spread as memes. If something is meant genuinely, but it is also crazy enough to be interpreted as a joke, people may reward it with "likes" and other engagement because they find it funny. Meanwhile, if something ironic is interpreted as genuine, people will be offended by it, which then also drives engagement as a form of ragebait. Either way, "edgy" humor is able to worm its way into the mainstream via the algorithm.

The "Oxford study" meme is a perfect example of Poe's law. Many of the commenting "trolls" seemed to be normal people who didn't have any knowledge of the meme's origins. They thought the serious blackpilled talking point was a funny joke about relationships, and they used it without understanding its harmful effects on Asian women. Later, more people assumed the study was real and interpreted the Oxford study jokes as serious, simultaneously furthering its unironic use.

Incels themselves often introduce serious topics as jokes, which can normalize their idea until it is revealed in its entirety. You start out laughing at how funny a "walkpilled cardiomaxxer" meme is, and then all of a sudden your For You page is dominated by incel memes, bringing you closer to the ideology.

You can see this in how their language has spread. I think it's pretty clear that the word "Chad" started out as a humorous archetype, but at a certain point incels began using it as a genuine classification to parallel the "beta" and "incel" social tiers. Then those tiers appeared so ridiculous to outsiders that they were able to spread as memes beyond *their* serious usage. Now we have people using the "Chad" and "virgin" characters as if they were stock characters in a new commedia dell'arte.

Poe's law has created a dangerous game of hopscotch. We're jumping between irony and reality, but we're not always sure where those lines are. Interpreting words comedically helps the algorithm spread them as memes and trends, but then interpreting them seriously manifests their negative effects.

. . . . . . . .

I want to make clear that the trend toward incel language is more than an extreme case study: It's an indicator of the linguistic changes happening on modern social media. The pipeline from 4chan to Reddit to TikTok is a perfect demonstration of how words move across platforms in ways that don't seem initially obvious.

Most of the algospeak examples from the first chapter had their own histories before being adopted to evade algorithmic censorship, and many of them followed the same path. For example, the earliest known mention of the word "seggs" was in a meme shared on 4chan's Pokémon discussion board in 2013. It was on that platform where the word began trending, before eventually spreading to Twitter and getting adopted on TikTok in 2020.

Meanwhile, the word "unalive" also started in 2013, coming from a widely shared Reddit meme drawing on a scene from *Ultimate Spider-Man*. These terms are popular in social media algospeak today only because of the early confluence of media and memes on other platforms that eventually diffused to mainstream TikToks.

When I talk about the linguistic "innovators" and "majority adopters" in diffusion-of-innovations theory, this is it. The innovators are always niche communities with shared interests and shared needs to create words. The reason we have so many words from incels is that they had an imperative to come up with new language for their common experiences, just as 4chan at large provided us with the terms "shitpost," "seggs," and "rickroll" because they had their own community with a need to invent slang.

In meme circles, it's a common aphorism that "all internet culture is downstream of 4chan," and evidence suggests this is at least partially true. In 2018, researchers at University College London used a technique called pHashing to trace where visually similar online images come from, and they found that a plurality of internet memes come from political forums on 4chan and Reddit.* They theorized that these communities are so pro-

---

* A Know Your Meme analysis also found this to be true for the 2010s, but noted that most new memes by 2022 were coming from TikTok or Twitter.[5]

lific at disseminating ideas because they intentionally weaponize memes as a form of "attention hacking," mixing funny templates with certain messages to further their ideologies.[6] If this is the case, then it's not that surprising that incel words have become so widespread. A huge part of their online virality was designed that way to spread the blackpill. Misery loves company; that's why the incels in my Reddit chat were so keen on converting us. When you combine their evangelizing zeal with their unique need to create words, the influx of extremist memes simply makes sense.

The incel moment in our pop culture is a testament to the power of memes in spreading words and ideas. By this point, we've been conditioned to consume information only if it's somehow funny or relatable. Studies suggest that nearly 90 percent of millennials mistrust traditional advertising tactics, and the numbers are even higher with Gen Z. The kind of messaging that worked on older generations is a tactic of the past: Anyone trying to push an idea or agenda today must rely on comedy. The best advertising is being done either through influencers (lending products a more organic feel) or through "unhinged" corporate accounts like Duolingo's, which openly leans into the meme that its mascot will hurt you if you don't complete your daily lesson. Through meme marketing, the company has been able to establish itself as one of the largest corporate presences on Instagram and TikTok, because it understands exactly how to hack into younger people's attention. The same is true for extreme ideologies like lookism: They diffuse best through memes.

Ironically, Duolingo has even leaned into these memes on several occasions: It has posted videos of its mascot mewing, joked about making a "brainrot" course to teach you the word "sigma," and published Duolingo "Chad" fan art. It had to play into these themes because that's how you connect to viewers today. I'm guilty of the same thing: Some of my most successful videos talk about words like "sigma" and "Chad," because I knew they would do well.

The unique spread of incel language further speaks to the power of the internet in enabling these ideas in the first place. In researching this chapter, I stumbled across an almost self-aware post on an incel forum that perfectly captures what I mean. "Imagine if the internet was never invented," the anonymous user begins. Then he goes on:

> I mean think about it no internet means you never ever visit this forum, which means you never get to become black-pilled and will probably be bluepilled and cucked and a beta simp for the rest of your life like how you were before you entered this forum. . . . And of course without the net incels would have no way to stage an effective incel rebellion because there would be zero alternative effective mass communication methods.[7]

Although I don't plan on making a habit of agreeing with incels, I think this poster got it right on the money. The internet first provided a medium for this community to form. It then gave them social media platforms to spread their ideas and attempt to start their "incel rebellion." The internet, and the engagement optimization algorithms that control it, have fomented stupid misinformation, extremist rhetoric, and dangerous frameworks that push their way into our everyday thoughts and speech.

The underlying linguistic process is nothing new. We know that K-pop groups use language to show in-group status and belonging. Even anime fans have a murky boundary between satirical and genuine slang, which is how phrases like *sussy baka* could spread, making fun of the anime community. Swifties, too, are stronger because the internet gave their subculture a space and helped their concepts spread through emergent trends.

But the internet has a shorter memory on short-form video platforms than ever before. We forget when we're joking and when we're telling the truth. We consume and disseminate memes without knowing where they originally came from, potentially furthering harmful ideas through our ignorance. The same patterns are playing out across all filter bubbles on social media—and, as we'll see in the next chapter, this doesn't just mean that communities can harm us. It means that we can harm communities.

## It's Giving Appropriation

I N THE 1940s, America began learning how to be cool.

The concept of a "cool" attitude had already been around in a non-temperature sense for decades—the earliest recorded usage of this definition traces back to the 1880s—but the word had previously been used only as an in-group term for speakers of African American English (AAE). To the Black community, to be "cool" was more than being fashionable or likable: It represented a general demeanor of calmness or stoicism in adverse situations.

The Yale professor Robert Thompson theorizes that this connotation can be traced back to the West African concept of *itutu*, an aesthetic of beauty and calmness similarly associated with cold temperature. In Yoruba and Igbo society, *itutu* represented nonchalance in difficult situations, and this cultural attitude directly translated to art and expression in a segregated America; someone who was "cool" comported themselves attractively while subtly defying oppression.[1] This carried over to jazz, which was defined by a "cool" attitude popularized through albums like Charlie Parker's *Cool Blues* and Miles Davis's *Birth of the Cool.* Soon, other counterculture communities like punks and beatniks started using the term—drawing on the same concept of detachment from the status quo.

Suddenly everybody wanted to be cool. Derivative expressions flourished: "cool cat," "keep your cool," "chill out." The idea of "cool" became alluring due to its exclusivity. Everybody started calling things cool or trying to be cool in some way, while the original artistic aesthetic shifted from niche use in the Black community to reflect an increasingly commercialized fashion ideology of wearing confident attire.

Ironically, the perception of coolness is exactly what made the word "cool" spread in the first place. Since the term served to build in-group status for socially desirable subcultures, those adjacent to or interested in the subcultures began using it to feel like part of the group. However, once the word became mainstream, it started gradually losing cultural value to the Black community. While still an important concept, it no longer reflected in-group status and no longer alluded to awareness of systematic racism. That notion had to be expressed through other words such as "hip" and "woke"—both of which were also eventually repurposed by outside communities.

The creation of "cool" and other AAE "slang" words was inherently cool under the original definition: The new vocabulary served as a concealed act of resistance against the straight white norms of the English language. As we learned in chapter 2, the idea of a "correct" English language emerged from the upper-class East Midlands dialect of the U.K.—a dialect that didn't represent the African diaspora in America, and yet one that was imposed on them. By creating new words for just themselves, the Black community has been able to reclaim their linguistic power. There remains a pressing social need to create new words, which is why white people have created proportionally less slang over the past hundred years.

And yet, because Black culture remains "cool" in the American popular consciousness, much of its in-group vocabulary ends up being subsumed by general culture. AAE words, though stigmatized because they go against the accepted "standard" culture, are paradoxically seen as having linguistic prestige precisely *because* they're part of the counterculture. As a result, they are borrowed by ever more mainstream groups until they're finally normalized, at which point the in-group must make new words.

This is the inevitable cycle of linguistic appropriation. When I say "appropriation," I simply mean "repurposing by a different social group"; the definition is often politically charged in culture-war arguments because it's inextricable from the social implications that follow.

Although the appropriation of African American English has occurred since at least the word "cool," this pattern has skyrocketed in the digital age. My rule of thumb for online slang is that if a word doesn't come from 4chan, it's probably from AAE, and it's shocking how frequently that holds true. Starting with Vine, the words "bae," "fleek," and "fam" all went from specific AAE origins to being called "Gen Z slang" or "internet slang." On modern platforms, this has only accelerated. Whenever we accuse someone of "speaking like TikTok," we're usually talking about specific grammatical constructions like "not you," "it's giving," and "the way you $X$"—all of which trace back to African American English, and all of which were adopted because they felt "cool." The same is true for a wide range of up-and-coming vocabulary words, including "cap," "sis," "bruh," and "bussin."

. . . . . . . .

Black vocabulary never enters general usage spontaneously. Rather, it follows the conduits of popularity much like any other social phenomenon, journeying from niche in-group usage to progressively peripheral circles until everyone is finally "in" on the reference.

This cycle is perhaps best illustrated through the rise of ball culture. Originally an underground LGBTQ movement, the "ballroom scene" evolved in predominantly Black and Latino dance circles in New York City in the 1980s and 1990s. It was an unapologetically queer space, characterized by extravagant pageantry, an elaborate "voguing" dance style, and flashy drag competitions. Resistance was central, just as with jazz. It was a resistance to gender norms—hence the drag—and a resistance to racism, which pervaded the few integrated spaces they previously had access to. Even queer Black joy was an act of resistance; it was an opportunity to celebrate identity in a way that challenged the white, cisgender norm of expression.

Ball culture was more than dance and more than drag. The communities it formed, known as *houses*, provided food and shelter to those on the edges of society. The families these houses formed were led by "mothers" and "fathers" who supported gay and transgender youth, often cast out by their families. Competitions were a way to earn prestige for one's house and further reinforce their important support systems. The act of dance itself carried special weight in the context of the raging AIDS epidemic and the history of BIPOC resistance.

Like any marginalized in-group, ball culture formed a unique vocabulary to signal a sense of belonging and to build identity. To subtly disrespect someone was to "throw shade." To demonstrate fierce femininity was to "give cunt." To show immense talent or beauty was to "slay," "work," "serve," or "eat it." Gossip was "tea"; shocking someone was "gagging" them; successful performers were "icons" or "queens"; and yes was "yass." If those terms seem familiar, it's because they're now all thought of as "internet slang." (If they don't seem familiar, then you probably don't consume short-form video content.)

How did this happen? How did the highly specialized argot of a niche subculture make its way out of New York City and into the lexicon of white teenage girls everywhere?

Mass media played an important role. Early songs and films, like Madonna's "Vogue" and the documentary *Paris Is Burning,* were critical for preserving the nascent culture. Later, TV shows, especially *RuPaul's Drag Race,* continued to popularize ball to larger groups and normalize its slang within gay and gay-adjacent groups, regardless of whether they were connected to the original Black and Latino houses.

*RuPaul's* peak viewership coincided with, and likely influenced, TikTok's surging interest in ball culture. Users in the early 2020s would post videos of themselves doing vogue dance moves like the duck walk or the death drop and using ball language like "slay" and "serve." As more and more people began appropriating the moves and terminology—often without crediting their sources—the connection to ballroom began to be lost.[2]

New media such as HBO's *Legendary* and Beyoncé's *Renaissance* emerged in an attempt to preserve and pay homage to the original movement. Intended to celebrate ball culture, these outlets played an important part in the gay community but inadvertently continued to popularize its language to wider audiences. Other media, like Meghan Trainor's 2023 hit "Mother" (opening with a man calling her "literally mother right now"), had far more tangential connections to the community. Never mind that the word once had the implication of a matronly drag queen who would protect others in her house. The term, like all the others, had evolved. Social media ate it up and began talking about how people "ate" it up.

By this point, out-groups had completely taken over the narrative; ball language was fully thought of as internet slang. In some cases, words' origins were erroneously attributed to other niche communities like stan culture: Swifties, for example, would often call Taylor Swift "mother," while K-pop fans would talk about how their favorite idols "gave cunt." Meanwhile, many in the original ballroom community felt an increasing disconnect with what had once been their own language.

There were some attempts to push back. Many in the queer BIPOC community were quick to point out the false equation of "drag" culture with "ball" culture, or to criticize people for "noguing" online instead of correctly "voguing," but the inexorable mainstreaming of their lifestyle had a mind of its own.

Just as the word "cool" had moved from African American English to General American English, ballroom slang permeated real and virtual filter bubbles in what should now be a highly predictable manner. First, it started with a highly niche group of "innovators" with a pressing social need to create new language. These innovators—here the members of the 1980s ball houses—came up with new words as a social reaction to their adverse living conditions and institutional oppression. Then, because it was perceived as especially "cool" or counterculture even in queer circles, ball slang moved to broader gay usage, including those uninvolved in the original ballroom scene. Finally, because gay people were seen as cool by young women, the slang terms diffused even further to those young women, losing context and meaning along the way. (An early drag queen would never have called Meghan Trainor "mother.") "Slay," for example, became more of a back-channeling response used by straight girls to react to things, the same way you might say "cool" to passively acknowledge something. Nowadays, that association makes the word feel awkward to a lot of queer Black people.

Each progression to a wider filter bubble arose in the pursuit of prestige, but was catalyzed by online spaces like TikTok.

A 2010 study from the UT Austin School of Journalism found that minorities tend to create more digital content, specifically with the intent to connect to their communities.[3] This and similar research suggest that early use of ball slang might have proliferated online for the same reason it was created in the real world: to build in-group community among the "early adopters." However, that same medium turned their in-group language into mainstream trends, as it so often does with all kinds of communities.

It bears repeating that social media is particularly effective in spreading these kinds of words due to the fuzzy boundaries of filter bubbles. "Slay" and "mother" spread because people thought it was okay to use those words, and they thought it was okay because they either felt like part of the in-group or they didn't understand the full context.

This feeling of periphery does exist in person: The reason straight girls adopt gay slang more quickly than straight boys is that girls tend to feel closer to the gay community, and are thus more okay with using their language. This feeling, however, has been exacerbated by the dissolution of cultural and ethnic barriers online. The online space makes in-groups feel more accessible by exposing users to more social circles than in real life, and then removes any regulatory ability from the original circles. If you were a straight white girl saying "slay" to someone in a real ball house in the 1990s, you likely would have gotten some funny looks and learned that the word wasn't meant for you to say (then again, you likely wouldn't have even known someone in a ball house). Today, it's harder to tell when the vibe is off. You see ballroom videos online and feel as if they were speaking to you even when the intent was to speak to others in their in-group. Now you feel a connection to that group, but they have no connection back to you—and no ability to tell you when an appropriation is inappropriate. Today, even if you *do* say "slay" in a video, it's going to reach people even further from the original community, with even less reason to believe they shouldn't *also* say "slay."

The fast pace of how words travel along increasingly adjacent social networks begets ignorance or misconceptions about where the words came from in the first place. Since most users first hear ballroom slang in out-of-context situations (being used by people who had already appropriated the slang), they feel okay using the words and further perpetuate the cycle. By the time we reached the point of middle-schoolers saying stuff like "yass queen," the words were well and truly dissociated from their original contexts. In fact, many people might feel threatened when confronted by the implication that the word isn't *theirs,* both because the concept of word ownership seems foreign and because by then it *does* feel as if it were theirs—they probably encountered it from other people like themselves.

· · · · · · · ·

In 2010, Unicode introduced the 🅱 emoji as part of a character series representing the four blood type groups. The symbol was largely unused, save for a few niche communities that found their own applications for it. One of those communities happened to be the Bloods street gang from Los Angeles, whose members routinely replaced the letter *c* in words to show disrespect to the rival Crip gang. For example, "clumsy" would become "🅱lumsy" and "confident" would become "🅱onfident."

Specialized gang vocabulary like this is quite common. Much as incels created unique words to build an exclusive in-group, gangs tend to create slang differentiating themselves from other gangs. This both builds internal identity and can be weaponized as "anti-language" targeting other gangs, as in the case of 🅱.

Although linguistic quirks are treated seriously in the organized crime world, they can also serve as a source of existential comedy for those living in gang-affected areas. To the mainly Black community dealing with Blood and Crip gang violence, the ironic use of the B emoji became a way to cope or poke fun at their difficult living situation. These memes made their way onto Black Twitter and eventually meme forums on Reddit, where non-Black people appropriated the character as a funny way to rewrite words. Suddenly white memelord teenagers started using it to replace any letter, especially in the context of writing "ni B B a" as a more acceptable way of saying the n-word. Once the joke became edgy and unfunny, its original power of mocking gang language was reduced in its communities of origin.[4]

Nevertheless, the semiotic train had left the station. Newly propelled by the success of the B memes, an entire genre of "hood irony" humor began to grip the internet by the mid-2010s. Since the Crip gang had a habit of replacing the letters *ck* with *cc* (*CK* had a connotation of "Crip killer"), the words "thick," "suck," and "fuck" began being humorously respelled as "thicc," "succ," and "fucc." Some of these are still used as algospeak substitutions; others have taken on their own lives, as with "succ" influencing the nickname "Zucc" for Mark Zuckerberg. And since the words "blood," "cuh," and "vro" were popular terms of endearment in various gangs, people began using them online as funny synonyms of "bro."

Perhaps the most popular and least obvious of these gang terms was the word "opp"—a clipping of "opponent" or "opposition" that emerged from the Chicago gang scene in the 2010s. After being popularized by Chicago-based rappers like Chief Keef, "opp" began being used in hood irony phrasal templates like "if you do *X*, consider yourself an opp." Eventually, the term made its way onto short-form video apps like TikTok, where it was widely accepted as Gen Z slang. With a seemingly surface-level etymology, very few people were ever made aware of the term's origin in gang culture. They didn't know they were making light of a serious topic still affecting many communities struggling with violence, and they didn't know they had appropriated language being used to process that. They had inadvertently taken and repurposed funny-sounding words from victimized groups without ever having to deal with those groups' struggles.

The "hood irony" meme genre is a microcosm of a larger effect: the problematic, underlying idea of Black culture being thought of as "funny." Studies show that people tend to find it humorous when a word has a less familiar spelling or origin. That's why there's an element of comedy when the Terminator says, "Hasta la vista, baby," or why English speakers sometimes jokingly say "adiós" or "no problemo" to each other. The same thing is happening with African American English language, which many white people find funny due to their lack of familiarity with it.

The word "gyat," for instance, reached social media as a funny word for "butt," but it actually comes from an exaggerated AAE pronunciation of "goddamn." Because the pronunciation was seen as amusing, it grew to be an ironic exclamation for seeing an attractive butt, eventually coming to serve as a noun for "butt" due to the association. By the point when it became "internet brainrot slang"—"sticking out your gyat for the Rizzler"—the word had been stretched and diluted in a way that ultimately made a farce of its original use. What's more, people have even created false etymologies for it: Two top results on Urban Dictionary claim that "gyat" stands for "girl you ate that" or "girl your ass thick." These kinds of "backronyms" harmfully reduce knowledge of where words actually come from, but are unfortunately unavoidable with modern slang.

A similar example is the word "ahh" instead of "ass," which was put on the map as part of the phrase "goofy ahh" in the early

2010s. This exaggerated pronunciation was most likely modeled on a southern dialect of African American English, although it's hard to tell for sure, because few people actually talk like that. At the very least, there was a *perception* that the word was AAE, since it also spread through hood irony memes until being extended to an "*X* ahh" phrasal template that became very popular for a brief span on TikTok and YouTube Shorts. By then, that association seems to have been forgotten: When I made a video on "ahh," numerous commenters "corrected" my pronunciation to "aw," showing that they not only were unaware of its origins but had further corrupted the original articulation.

As with all memes, joke appropriations are often quite short and tied to trends. And as someone who posts daily videos on TikTok and Instagram, I always notice the same pattern playing out in my comments section: A joke seems funny, gets good interaction, and is then reused until it becomes stale and eventually forgotten about. For a solid week in March 2024, my top comment would always be something along the lines of "etymology ahh video." Later, for about a week in April, my top comment was always "If you don't fuck with etymologynerd, consider yourself an opp." While I appreciated that sentiment, I couldn't help but notice how quickly these jokes went from fresh to overdone. Pieces of Black culture were being treated as entertainment to the point where they were no longer thought of as Black culture, before eventually being discarded. Meanwhile, the inescapably "social media" or "Gen Z" associations cast onto the words took them out of the hands of marginalized communities who had started those jokes as a form of power.

In videos when I point this out, I always get commenters offended at the implication that they're complicit in linguistic appropriation. As with ballroom slang, they heard the word from someone else, *they* aren't at fault for how it's being used, and well, why should anyone be allowed to police *their* language?

This reaction and attitude ironically reflects the extent to which the words have diffused from their initial origins; it's honestly an impressive testament to modern etymology that angry white forty-year-olds are arguing that the words "gyat" and "ahh" belong to them. In reality, nobody is actually trying to police those words: This is a gut reaction from someone who either doesn't fully understand what's happening or is uncomfortable admitting that their use of slang can be harmful.

"Gyat" and "ahh," for example, both exaggerate African American English pronunciation. Most dialects don't pronounce the words "god" or "ass" that way, and yet those were the versions popularized on social media because they seemed funnier. The underlying intent still fits in with the out-group pursuit of being "cool," but this time it was only through the medium of comedy.

While the people popularizing these words most likely didn't mean harm, they're unintentionally responsible for reinforcing racist stereotypes of Black people as overly expressive or dramatic. Since the era of nineteenth-century minstrel theater, AAE has been parodied through distorted language, in a way that still affects the American racial climate today. Because of burlesque words like "gyat," "ahh," and other respellings like "periodt" for "period," people are more likely to write off AAE slang as "incorrect," or to believe in misinformed generalizations about African Americans.

Even outside written language, our visual representations often play into these tropes: Studies have shown that non-Black people are disproportionately likely to use reaction GIFs and images containing Black people, because they find those memes funnier. If you've ever been sent the "Crying Michael Jordan" or "Michael Jackson Eating Popcorn," those subtly play into racial stereotypes by using Black reactions as an exaggerated response. This phenomenon is called *digital blackface,* and it's very present in the social media age.[5]

In 2023, the Black community on TikTok began criticizing the Asian American creator Tray Soe for speaking in a "Blaccent"—a fake African American English accent used by non-Black individuals to mimic Black people. Instead of saying "corn bread," for instance, Tray would say "cone bread," which she attributed to her Atlanta upbringing despite nobody in Atlanta speaking that way. Although she initially denied exaggerating her accent, Tray's earlier YouTube videos revealed that she had previously spoken in a very different, stereotypically influencer-style accent. Just as she had likely adopted the influencer accent to fit in earlier, Tray was probably imitating AAE to tap into its perceived coolness and to appear closer to Black culture.

Danielle Bainbridge, an assistant professor at Northwestern University, points out in an episode of *PBS Origins* that the "Blaccent" has been around for more than a century and has always been characterized by an imbalance of power. White artists, from Elvis to Billie Eilish, have seen huge profits from adopting a palatable "Black" affectation for the American public, while comparable Black artists have been criticized for those same linguistic patterns without seeing the same success. In the digital world, though, this is even more common. Unless someone is speaking with blatantly exaggerated pronunciations like "cone bread," it can be difficult to tell where certain styles of speaking come from—which leads us to bastardizations like "gyat" and "ahh." Professor Bainbridge argues that this equation of "internet lingo" with the Blaccent is a "slippery slope" normalizing the adoption and subsequent caricaturing of African American culture.[6]

........

Hood irony and ballroom slang are just two small examples of African American English coming into the mainstream. They're also extremely different examples of what it means to *speak*

African American English, capturing radically different fragments of the Black experience that have been lumped together for convenience. You would never hear a member of the Crips gang saying "werk, queen," just as you would never see a drag queen use the B emoji. This is because African American English is not a monolith, but rather is composed of many subdialects, which reflect the many different Black subcommunities.

Both instances are, however, characterized by outside groups profiting off another culture by using in-group language for their own benefit. When a company like Duolingo makes videos with the words "gyat" and "slay," it seems cooler than other companies that aren't caught up on modern slang, which has been a huge part of its marketing strategy. But this means that Duolingo is commodifying and profiting off appropriations of African American English, without any input from the original groups.

Admittedly, group input is hard when the group is poorly defined and the word has been out of their hands for a while. Not *all* words come from groups, however; this can also have an impact on a more tangible, individual level.

In 2014, the Vine user Kayla Newman went viral for coining the word "fleek" in a video where she brags about her "eyebrows on fleek." The video was remixed countless times, and then, according to an interview she did with BET, "it took a week for the celebrities to get hold of it." Personalities like Ariana Grande and Kim Kardashian started using the phrase on social media. IHOP and Taco Bell got Twitter likes for calling their food "on fleek." Forever 21 and H&M sold "fleek" T-shirts. Nicki Minaj rapped about being "pretty on fleek," then publicly feuded with another celebrity who sold "pretty on fleek" T-shirts without cutting her a percentage of the profits.

Kayla, of course, never received her own royalties, despite having actually come up with the term. Under copyright law, she technically did own the rights to her video, but in a more practical sense it's very difficult to control your content once it gets online. While most social media companies will honor requests to remove copyrighted content, their terms and conditions also disavow responsibility for intellectual property theft, meaning that it can be a challenge to control the spread of something once it's replicated—and that's just for a full video. Words are even more slippery: You can't claim copyright just for coining a phrase. Kayla tried on several occasions to trademark "on fleek," but by the time the phrase died out a few years later, the corporations and celebrities had already cashed out on its popularity.[7]

And why would anyone pay Kayla for saying "fleek" anyway? The question of ownership is tricky, especially online. After her initial video, the word went viral in its own right, being repurposed in other trending contexts and becoming regarded as just another piece of "internet slang," as opposed to being something that the creator should be paid for.

The trend-based nature of how memes are remixed directly causes this loss of ownership. Popular words never stay in a single meme or expression for long, but are instead reapplied to many different contexts; this is inherently what helps make them popular in the first place. As the words are reapplied, however, they're increasingly dissociated from their initial settings until their origins are forgotten. This simply makes sense from a mathematical perspective: If only 50 percent of people reposting a meme credit its origin, then only 25 percent will credit it in the second round of sharing, and so on.

In reality, the number is much lower than 50 percent. People very rarely think about online attribution when they're sharing content. They think about themselves and the people they're sharing it with, which is perfectly normal, but that means that the person or group that created it is left out. I did this sometimes when I began posting on Reddit: I would find trending images on other websites and repost them simply because they would help me go viral. It didn't occur to me that I should've been attributing sources until much later, when larger accounts started reposting my own original content and I felt upset about being left out of the attention.

I get it, though: Giving credit can be cumbersome and paradoxically make a post less likely to succeed. Recall the Reddit post "Snowfall in Sequoia National Park, California," and how it would sound less compelling as "Snowfall in Sequoia National Park, California, by X photographer"; the latter gives too much information and is worse at creating a curiosity gap. Your posts will also do better when there's plausible deniability that *you* took the picture. Even though the first option doesn't directly claim ownership, it will likely get more upvotes because some people will nevertheless believe it's original content and reward it as such. On video platforms, people's attention spans are even shorter, with that effect becoming more pronounced.

It's also far more intuitive to give credit to an entire photo or video than some small part of it, which may be why Kayla Newman received especially little recognition for "on fleek." When someone remakes a trend in their own fashion, they feel their own sense of ownership and attachment to that version.

In the early days of TikTok, the budding influencer Charli D'Amelio exploded in popularity for her rendition of the Renegade, an energetic dance originally choreographed and performed by Jalaiah Harmon, a fourteen-year-old from Atlanta. Even though Jalaiah invented the dance, she received zero credit from other creators, while Charli went on to become known as the "CEO of Renegade" and raked in millions from subsequent sponsorships.

Although Charli did have to deal with online backlash and eventually apologized for her video, she had already reaped the profits of Jalaiah's work—which illustrates a broader trend in social media of larger accounts benefiting from smaller accounts, with little recognition for the smaller accounts. Larger accounts take what is "cool," put their own spin on it, and usually publish that without giving credit, since credit doesn't feel "cool" or intuitive to give. Just as with dances, this happens whenever someone coins a word.

........

As I work on this chapter, the AAE words I write about keep getting spell-checked or autocorrected, because they're not seen as "standard English." Instead, they're dismissed as "incorrect," based on the idea that the East Midlands–derived dialect of English is the "correct" one. Beyond spell-check, I keep seeing this attitude in my comments section whenever I talk about new AAE-derived words. There's always someone bemoaning the "corruption of the English language" or saying that the slang words irritate them because they're "grammatically wrong."

In reality, of course, "correct" English is a construct. The purpose of language is simply to be understood, and people can get their point across in many different ways. Even "correct" English is constantly shifting, borrowing words from "incorrect" dialects. The word "cool" used to be thought of as slang, but was eventually accepted as standard once its AAE origins were forgotten. Then we had to find new terms to criticize, and so the cycle of linguistic gentrification continues.

With modern slang in particular, new words are frequently written off as "brainrot" or "internet slang." In early 2024, an English teacher went viral for publishing a list of thirty-two slang words prohibited in her classroom, including "cap," "bet," "gyat," "it's giving," and "period"—all AAE vocabulary. "The gibberish some of you choose to use is improper English," she writes, threatening to make rule breakers write an essay explaining why they thought it was appropriate to use slang in school.

Even though African American English is constantly scrutinized, it's also constantly sought after. The very words being dismissed by the English teacher became popular *because* they were dismissed by the establishment, and therefore "cool" in both the original and the modern sense of the word. This is what makes people want to use them and spread them.

We can see this happening in real time, not only on social media, but also in the classroom. In a survey I conducted of more than two thousand middle school teachers and parents in July 2024, more than half reported hearing their children use the ballroom words "yass," "tea," "slay," "queen," "giving," and "ate." Of my respondents, 91 percent think their children are learning these words through social media. At the same time, they've taken on an important function offline: Eighty-four percent of the parents and teachers are sure that kids are using these words because their friends use them, while 57 percent believe they serve a community-building function. This shows that ballroom slang is still being used as in-group vocabulary, just for a very different in-group than it once was. Beyond drag queens, "tea" and "ate" now create a shared identity for middle-schoolers.

While "coolness" is absolutely as much of a factor for Gen Alpha as it has been for previous generations, younger children especially tend to rely on comedy. "Gyat" was one of the most popular words in this time period, with more than three-quarters of the surveyed adults hearing it being used. This represents a huge increase from the 55 percent of teachers and parents who had heard it when I conducted a similar survey six months prior—and this represents only *adults* who *have* heard the word; surely the actual number is higher among children. Meanwhile, more than 60 percent of adults have heard hood irony slang like "opp," and agree that kids are using these words because they sound "funny." This leads to the association of these terms as mere jokes or Gen Alpha slang, potentially delegitimizing their place in African American English and leading to slang blacklists like the one from the English teacher mentioned earlier.

Whenever words spread, their etymology is forgotten and the vibe changes. Dialectal slang always gets reproduced and appropriated without credit, meaning that people will misattribute the source in the best-case scenario or exaggerate and change the words in the worst-case scenario. This happens more frequently online, since words enter our vocabularies faster and without any context. More than 85 percent of my surveyed parents and teachers are confident that their kids are unaware that at least some of their slang words are AAE, but it's not just the kids who are unaware; it's society at large.

Internet culture goes hand in hand with stealing ideas, but those ideas sometimes carry important social capital that gets lost with each new iteration. Once people finally do forget where a word comes from, it either gets discarded as passé (like "fleek") or widely adopted as standard English (like "cool"). In either situation, it loses significance to the community that created it. It's stripped of its power—the very reason it was created in the first place.

# 8

..........

# What Are We Wearing This Summer?

I N THE EARLY DAYS of the internet, before machine learning algorithms dominated social media recommendations, the most important algorithm was far and away the search engine. The only way to have your website discovered was to stand out in search results, a goal that became ever trickier to reach in the growing expanse of information online. In response to this challenge, developers began enhancing their site's visibility by prioritizing certain searchable keywords.

When I wanted my etymology blog to rank higher in Google search results, for example, I put terms like "linguistics" and "etymology" in the site description so that Google would know to recommend it to people searching for etymology content. By including the kinds of phrases that people look up, developers are able to nudge algorithms into directing traffic toward their websites. This practice is known as *search engine optimization,* or SEO.

SEO remains incredibly important on social media. TikTok actively included "search value" as one of the four payment metrics when it introduced its Creator Rewards Program in 2024, since it wanted its videos to be discoverable by both its own search feature and other search engines like Google. Creators then respond to these types of incentives by including relevant titles, hashtags, and captions, but this barely scratches the surface of how modern algorithms rely on keywords.

The very reason we feed search engines metadata in the first place is that their algorithms require information to function. The more that can be categorized and tagged, the easier it is to rank the relevance of a web page. In the same way, social media algorithms are best at recommending personalized videos when we give them information. Since that translates to social media success, we create metadata simply because the algorithm *wants* metadata in order to push our content to others.

There is no better illustration of this phenomenon than the suffix "-core," used to denote a specific fashion aesthetic. Living a traditional or bucolic lifestyle, for example, is now called "cottagecore." Bright pink artificial vibes are "Barbiecore." A fluttery, mythological palette is "fairycore." The online Aesthetics Wiki lists over 150 more variations, with categories as bizarre as "grandmacore," "clowncore," and "traumacore."[1]

It wasn't always like this. The modern sense of the suffix can be traced back to a single word, "hardcore," which described a genre of 1970s punk music that was "hard to the core." From there, "-core" was clipped off and applied to other music genres like "emocore," "speedcore," and "gloomcore," occasionally extending to the visual aesthetics that accompanied those categories. It wasn't until early 2020, however, when the explosion of "-cores" really began. The vast majority of the 150 aesthetics— including absurd subgenres like monkeycore, captchacore, and plaguecore—didn't exist in a meaningful sense before the rise of short-form video platforms.

That's not a coincidence: Terms such as "cottagecore" and

"Barbiecore" now serve the same function as the words "etymology" and "linguistics" in my blog description. Beyond being mere fashion aesthetics, the "-cores" are an extremely specific way to tell the algorithm what kind of content to recommend to the viewer. The end goal still optimizes for user recommendation, but in this case it's just for algorithmic optimization instead of search engine optimization.

Before social media, if I wanted to describe my fashion aesthetic, I would have said that I generally preferred earth tones. Now I can get far more specific, clarifying whether my wardrobe is really "earthcore" or actually "campcore," "naturecore," or "goblincore"—all different "microlabels" you can find on social media.

In SEO terms, these new words would have meant that I can more quickly find the specific kind of earth-toned clothing I'm looking for (that is, I play an active role in using this word). In algorithmic optimization terms, they instead mean that I'll more frequently get recommended videos featuring my specific aesthetic (that is, I play a passive role in using this word). Each time I interact with a "goblincore" video, I'm more likely to be recommended other goblincore videos, since the algorithm uses that word knowing I will like and interact with similar content. Whether it appears in the title, hashtag, captions, or even comments, the algorithm picks up on my interest in "goblincore" and factors it in when determining if a video fits onto my feed. As a result, I'm pushed a little further into the goblincore community, making the content feel even more relevant.

The more specific these labels are, the better, because the algorithm is able to give you more personalized recommendations. It's simply easier for a machine to understand you if it can somehow categorize you, then compare you with people in similar categories. Creators know this and intentionally help spread or create these labels to give their videos a chance of being picked up by the algorithm. Just as "cringe" creators make content with the words "gyat," "rizz," and "skibidi" because they know those words are trending, the "aesthetic" creators make "cottagecore" content because they know that will also be pushed to a specific community.

Essentially, we are seeing so many of these fashion micro-labels pop up precisely because social media prioritizes them, and this has been happening with all kinds of online aesthetics beyond just the "-core" suffix. If you dress stereotypically feminine, you can be "coquette," "babygirl," or "soft girl." If you dress intellectually, you can be "dark academia," "light academia," "vintage academia," or one of fifty other labels on the Aesthetics Wiki. Whether you identify as "coastal cowgirl" or "acid pixie" or "clean girl," there is some kind of recently invented term out there to describe your specific sartorial preferences. The algorithm devours it all, waiting for you to like an aesthetic video so it can attach a label to you and understand you a little bit better.

This isn't isolated to fashion. Look at Spotify, which has created more than six thousand "microgenres" of music to better categorize audio information. If I wanted to, I could listen to "escape room" or "permanent wave" or "preverb"—all of which were invented to label newly categorized genres of music. In some cases, these microgenres have directly influenced how we talk about music: Even though the "bedroom pop" and "hyper-pop" genres had already been around in some capacity, Google Trends shows usage of the terms abruptly increasing after their respective Spotify debuts in 2018 and 2019.

To find out more, I interviewed Glenn McDonald, Spotify's former data alchemist and the guy behind most of those genres. Glenn thinks of his work as "finding communities." By grouping together similar songs and artists, his team was able to determine which communities each listener belonged to, whether they even knew those communities existed or not.

Although there isn't a single Spotify algorithm in the sense that we talk about a TikTok algorithm or YouTube algorithm for video recommendations, Glenn tells me that mapping out the genre space nevertheless helps Spotify better understand its own catalog. Aggregating music by genre makes it easier to answer questions like whether a particular song qualifies as "instrumental" or not.[*]

Spotify's algorithms don't even need to create and name genres in order to function: They can identify communities by just grouping common data patterns. Names are then ways for humans to understand what the algorithm did, but this circularly affects how we think and talk about those labels. Once Spotify put hyperpop on the map, for example, Glenn recounts intense "fights over what was hyperpop and not, with the Spotify playlist being part of that cultural argument." By even applying a descriptor in the first place, the app popularized and validated the genre.

The same thing is happening with the "-core" microlabels. As soon as "cottagecore" started trending on social media, creators responded by making more cottagecore content, with each additional video serving to normalize the emergent community. Suddenly social media had one more in-group to cater to, making the experience more specific—and therefore more engaging—to that group.

Aesthetics affect more than just your music and fashion sense; these words are packaged as entire *lifestyles*. If you're really a "cottagecore person," you're not going to stop at dressing cottagecore and listening to cottagecore artists like Lana Del Rey. You'll buy doilies and wallpaper to decorate your cottagecore house. You'll make old-fashioned meals by following cottagecore recipes. You'll consume cottagecore books and movies like *Little Women*

---

* He goes into more detail on this example in his fascinating book *You Have Not Yet Heard Your Favourite Song.*

and *The Secret Garden.* The words being spread by the algorithm now also serve as labels and metadata. At a certain point, the distinction breaks down, and the SEO terms can be extended to every domain of your life.

. . . . . . . .

SEO may still be important, but keywords do far more than just optimize for search the way they used to. They now optimize for *social media algorithms,* which in turn optimize for engagement by building in-groups whenever possible. The more communities that are created, the more targeted your feed is, and the more you engage because you feel as if the algorithm "really knows you."

Of course, labels have always been important for finding and building identity. In the past, you might've used labels to figure out whether you were a "goth" or a "punk", but now there are so many more options. Through just a little online exploration, you can more meticulously delineate whether you identify as "vampire goth," "pastel goth," "glam goth," or a retronymic "trad goth."

These identities didn't exist before social media. The internet has enabled people to discover more niche communities than they had access to in real life. If someone identified as a goth pre-internet but also liked pastel clothing, they wouldn't have known that "pastel goths" were a thing. Most of the other goths they interacted with would've fit under the broad "goth" label, but they'd be unlikely to find others with their exact fashion taste.

Then came the internet, and with it a built-in gathering place for people with geographically disparate interests. Finally, you'd be able to find other goths who like pastels, and you could form your own community around that aesthetic. With new identities come new words, and so websites like Tumblr created the label "pastel goth" in the early 2010s. Once TikTok came along, it further popularized the term, along with other niche Tumblr aesthetics like cottagecore.

As with "hyperpop," many fashion microlabels had already been around in niche communities, but they were largely unknown until being elevated into our collective consciousness through short-form video and its tendency to amplify subcultural vocabulary. Nevertheless, the very popularization of labels like "pastel goth" and "cottagecore" manifested those communities by giving them a named identity to rally around. In the same way that "punk" and "goth" helped people in the 1980s figure out which social bucket they belonged to, these new aesthetics do the same thing on a more compartmentalized scale today.

By legitimizing some identities, social media opens the door to even more identities. Early aesthetics like cottagecore spurred the development of the more niche "-cores" like grandmacore; occasionally, they would even generate tongue-in-cheek parodies like *corecore,* a postmodern aesthetic satirizing the other "-core" aesthetics.

However ridiculous they may be, each new identity directly increases value for social media platforms. Beyond creating more targeted filter bubbles and contributing to a sense of shared app culture, these terms pose invaluable marketing opportunities to businesses. Whenever an aesthetic community is formed, that community represents a new demographic that can be advertised to. The deeper you gravitate into the cottagecore filter bubble, for example, the more you identify with the cottagecore aesthetic and the more you want to buy cottagecore clothing to fit that new aesthetic.

As we now know, this comes down to the innate human inclination to join in-groups. Whenever somebody realized they identified as a goth in the past, they would buy more black clothing or goth makeup to better fit in. The same is true for the pastel goths of TikTok today—with the difference being that pastel goth clothing is now one click away on the TikTok shop, newly available through drop-shipping and large-scale internet fashion retailers.

The cycle viciously feeds into itself. The more people buy into an aesthetic, the more the community is built up and the easier it is for others to identify with that aesthetic. Not only are social media platforms aware of this phenomenon, but they actively incentivize it through integrated online shops and creator rewards. Influencers are offered eye-watering incentives to promote items being sold through the shops, lending them an organic advertising feel. When a cottagecore creator promotes "cottagecore" apparel online, that not only reinforces the cottagecore identity for others but also feels much more authentic than a traditional advertisement. In contrast to stilted, unnaturally scripted promotions, this style of "influencer marketing" makes it feel as though the cottagecore influencer were simply recommending a product they like to others in their community. Reality, of course, is different. Companies and platforms are partnering with an army of content-creating minions to maximize profit from the online identities they helped manufacture in the first place.

Interestingly, they're not even trying to hide this. A 2021 landing page for TikTok's business platform openly claims that "subcultures are the new demographics" and lays out advice for how to best capitalize on aesthetics like cottagecore and dark academia. It goes on to explicitly state the following:

> [Subcultures] personalize your approach, resulting in a stronger connection with customers. Your brand becomes part of their identity. TikTokers turn to subcultures to define their online and offline personas, which means they will actively seek out brands they can identify with and align to their true selves.[2]

TikTok is admitting a lot here, but I'm particularly drawn to the sentence "your brand becomes part of their identity." It's right there in black and white: Social media creates new identities in order to commodify them. One can easily forget that these platforms are *businesses first,* and everything they do is a reflection of their business priorities. If the algorithm spreads new words and identities that build communities, that's because the platform believes those communities will earn it more money in the end.

Beyond creating algorithmic identity, the hyper-compartmentalization of cultural labels is part of a retail strategy known as the *long-tail model,* wherein small quantities of unique items are sold to niche audiences. While most retailers are forced to market more general products that will appeal to larger demographics (the "head" of demand distribution), larger companies are able to utilize their economies of scale to sell increasingly

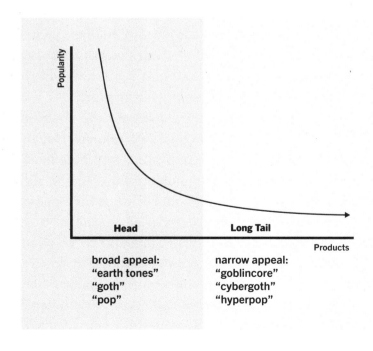

niche products (the "tail" of demand), which expands their consumer base while outpacing smaller competitors. This is how Amazon and Walmart are able to continuously push out small businesses: Their size allows them to offer more for cheaper, turning them into one-stop shops for both head and tail products.

In a 2004 *Wired* article identifying the concept, the author Chris Anderson contrasts Amazon with traditional booksellers like Barnes & Noble. While the average brick-and-mortar bookstore carries 130,000 highly popular titles, Amazon's catalog in 2004 already had *millions,* making the majority of its sales *outside* those 130,000 best-selling books. It was able to do that by stocking up on content for niche audiences and pushing that content to those audiences through personalized recommendations. Short-form video apps are doing the exact same thing with their identity-tailored products. The only difference is that the new apps are going so far as to *create and build* the identities they cater to.[3]

Scarcity isn't a problem in the digital age; every product is easily accessible. While a physical cottagecore store might not do that well in person, its digital equivalent will find customers regardless of geographic constraint. In Anderson's prescient words, "The future of business is selling less of more."

Now that Meta, ByteDance, and Alphabet have engineered these niche communities on Instagram, TikTok, and YouTube, they alone hold an advantage in controlling corporate marketing to their all-new "subcultural demographics." Their wealth of user data makes it easier to target products, while their platform shops are conveniently accessible to third-party sellers.

So what does this have to do with language? Well, all of it. This is all reflected in the language we use online, and increasingly in person. Each "goth" categorization and each new "-core" is an emergent effect of algorithmic business priorities intersecting with the human tendency to create in-groups. Each new aesthetic microlabel helps the algorithm know which terms best apply to us, which end up affecting our own aesthetic preferences, which further reinforce the algorithmic labels. Identities are interchangeable with metadata, and metadata is interchangeable with our everyday language.

........

The creator economy directly feeds into long-tail economics. Some influencers, such as Charli D'Amelio on TikTok and the streamer PewDiePie on YouTube, make incredibly general content appealing to wide audiences—the "head" of the demand curve for content. For users with more specific interests (say, a passion for linguistics), creators like me exist for highly specialized niches—the "tail" of the demand curve.

Though some creators are just on social media for fun or popularity, any creator trying to earn serious money on social media must fit themselves into a niche. Part of this is because their followers expect reliably similar content, but another key part of it is simply because we feel as if the algorithm pushes us into those niches. Platforms like TikTok make no secret that they want us to post consistent content: It's in every "advice for creators" bulletin they publish, and it's well known that the algorithm takes content similarity into account. When I post a linguistics video, it'll be pushed to people who have already liked my linguistics videos. But if I were to suddenly switch things up and post a makeup routine, the algorithm would figure that out from the metadata and not push the video to my reliable, known audience. It might go nowhere instead.

On Spotify, Glenn McDonald tells me that a lot of musicians "assume the tags are constraining," and thus choose to consign themselves to a particular style of music out of guesses about what the "algorithm" is looking for—often incorrectly. In the same way, a cottagecore influencer may make cottagecore content simply because they feel confined to that category, rather than making more general rural-themed content as they might have done before the label existed.

The other option is to jump on trends. Instead of just cottagecore content, an "aesthetic" creator can straddle the line between the head and the long tail by playing into whatever niche "-core" is trending in a particular moment (and there's always one trending). These influencers may make a goblincore video one day, then an angelcore video the next; in fact, they're often incentivized to. This is where fast fashion comes in.

Starting with brands like Zara in the late twentieth century, retailers began shifting away from durable, high-quality clothing and toward a higher output of cheaper, trend-based, replaceable apparel. Today, online brands have done the same thing on an even faster scale. E-commerce websites like Temu and Shein produce flimsy, unethically sourced products at extremely low cost in response to every social media microtrend. In researching this chapter alone, I almost got sucked into buying an admittedly gorgeous goblincore shirt for eight dollars on Shein.

Social media platforms are critical to the success of these companies. Both Temu and Shein broke through to U.S. markets with their "influencer hauls," where well-known fashion creators unbox packages of products. This remains a major advertising strategy, and it has a symbiotic relationship with social media's compartmentalization of identity. A quick search on TikTok reveals hundreds of videos showing off "Shein cottagecore hauls," reinforcing the concept of a cottagecore identity and "cottagecore" as a word itself in a circular, self-perpetuating way.

As soon as the short attention spans of social media shift to a new "-core" aesthetic, the fast-fashion retailers are ready to hop on the trend and sell products in that theme. Trends are good for them. The more trends, the more they can sell. The faster the trends happen, the faster they can sell.[4] In some cases, marketers even create trends.

A curious example of this is how we've recently started labeling our summers. All over social media, 2019 was universally acknowledged as "hot girl summer." 2023 was "Barbie summer," and 2024 was "brat summer." It wasn't always like this: The only other named summer before that was 1967's summer of love, but this feels different. "Hot girl" and "brat" served to advertise new music releases by Megan Thee Stallion and Charli XCX, while "Barbie" advertised a new film release. Labeling these time periods with products turned them into trends, and therefore made them more marketable.

Creators play into this pattern because, of course, it pays to hop onto social media trends. In the same way that influencers "trendbait" by coining neologisms like "girl dinner" and "Roman Empire," we're also rewarded if we identify and espouse emerging market trends online. Pay close attention at the start of June. You'll suddenly start noticing fashion creators asking the refrain "What are we wearing this summer?" or musicians telling us, "I think I just wrote the song of the summer." They have to do this. In an increasingly transitory internet landscape, attaching a product to a moment in time lends it a greater salience.[5] You can't blame them for trying.

Real creators are needed for the sense of authenticity to make a trend really take off, but that won't stop companies from trying to tap into the moment by associating a particular message with the summer zeitgeist. In 2019, Wendy's tried to brand its lemonade the "official drink" of hot girl summer, and so many other companies attempted to create their own summer trends that *The New York Times* wrote a 2023 article making fun of the "three-word Mad Lib" game being played with all the "adjective, noun, season" microtrends being thrown around.[6]

As that article pointed out, it only makes sense for the companies to be doing this because of the "tantalizing possibility of getting it right," for when it *does* go right, it goes *really* right. During Barbie summer, for instance, sales of Barbie-related items increased more than 100 percent, so it's no wonder that advertisers want to keep up.[7] Meanwhile, in politics, the 2024 Kamala Harris campaign saw a huge bump in popularity from successfully co-branding its candidate as synonymous with "brat summer." Within days of the Charli XCX album beginning to trend on social media, creators hopped onto the fad through Kamala-themed edits. "You think you just fell out of a coconut tree?" Kamala asks over a lime-green video of Charli's song "360," continuing with the line, "You exist in the context of all in which you live and what came before you."

The edits, a breath of fresh air after Biden's demoralizing decision to suspend his campaign, are exactly why everybody's always clamoring to have the "song of the summer" or decide "what we're wearing this summer." By striking when the iron is hot, marketers have a real chance of harnessing a collective label to create an organic-feeling social media phenomenon.[*]

Summer is always a prominent instance of how the boundary between words and branding campaigns can get blurred, but this is happening all over, especially on fashion TikTok. I'm particularly drawn to the word "preppy," which dramatically shifted in meaning since the rise of recommendation algorithms. While older generations still associate the term with the upper-class style of American "preparatory" schools (from whence the word came), it's taken on a completely new function for Gen Alpha: describing bright, stereotypically girly clothing.

Despite hearing a lot about the new "preppy" through my research, I almost didn't believe it myself, and had to text my eleven-year-old cousin to confirm—but confirm she did. Preppy

---

[*] Notably, this is a double-edged sword: By tying Kamala Harris to a trend, her campaign turned her into yet another fad that became less popular as the summer ended.

things "have to be very pink and vivid," she tells me. She goes on to describe it as the "brighter stuff and the newest stuff."

How did this happen? How did the word shift so dramatically in meaning in such a short time span? It all has to do with how the label was captured and co-opted by more mainstream brands. Although "preppy" started in the catalogs of upscale retailers such as Ralph Lauren and Brooks Brothers, it soon began being offered by youth-targeted fast-fashion stores like Aeropostale and Hollister. These retailers marketed "preppy" at an affordable price to "basic" upper-middle-class girls, who turned the term into more of a buzzword of what they like to wear. Suddenly "preppy" was anything that was popular with the popular girls, and that typically meant bright pink clothing.

By itself, this was a pretty normal shift. Words change meanings like this all the time through a normal linguistic process known as *semantic drift*. The other part of the equation, however, was more deliberate: The word was intentionally captured by companies trying to profit off a trending word. Though kickstarted by brands like Hollister, the transition really happened because of smaller boutique stores like the Texas-based dear hannah, prep and the New York City–based cutandcropped (both stylized in lowercase), each of which has built up hundreds of thousands of social media followers by marketing its bright, girly apparel as "preppy clothing."

The top video on cutandcropped's TikTok account, with almost two million views, opens with the owner describing the "least favorite thing in my preppy shop," then showing off a cute smiley-face tote bag, then ending with the sentence "available in my TikTok shop now." The video description sports the metadata #preppy, #preppyaesthetic, and seven other preppy-related hashtags, while the account bio describes itself as the "preppiest shop in New York City." Simply put, the video was a masterpiece of algorithmic optimization. The owner of cutandcropped didn't care what baby boomers thought the definition of "preppy" was. She knew her audience (teenage girls), and she knew that this was a trendy word for that demographic. She used the label in her video hook, in her video description, and consistently across her account because she knew it would be recommended to people who had previously shown interest in "preppy clothing." After capitalizing on the trending word, she made sure to integrate her product into the TikTok shop to make it easier. With enough brands doing this, the definition of "preppy" genuinely changed among younger generations. If you can't coin a new word, just hijack an old one.

The video's hashtags were only one method of algorithmic optimization. Every time the word "preppy" was spoken aloud or shown on-screen, the algorithm also picked up on that and factored it in, which shows how far marketing language has moved beyond simple SEO. Even regularly spoken language can now hyper-specify a brand to its intended audience, and the cutandcropped account took full advantage of that.

While writing this, I realized I lived twenty minutes away from the physical cutandcropped location, so I walked over on a whim to speak with its owner, Sophie. Interestingly, she tells me that the idea of "preppy" wasn't something she thought she would be capitalizing on. Starting out on TikTok, she knew only the old sense of the word, until she realized her younger audience was commenting on how her cheerfully maximalist items looked "preppy."

That's when Sophie fully embraced it, rebranding her social media presence and releasing a new line of products to fit the aesthetic. "It was important for me to lean into that idea and use that word all the time," she tells me. "I knew for that hashtag we would come up at the top because it's a new term."

She's right. When you search "preppy stores in New York City," cutandcropped is usually the first option, since it successfully optimized for a trending algorithmic keyword. "It's like a whole new demographic of people who like colorful, fun, cute things," she says, unknowingly echoing the TikTok business platform's phrasing.

Over the course of our interview, I couldn't help but notice that Sophie used the terms "word," "hashtag," and "demographic" interchangeably when talking about the concept of "preppy." Why would she separate them, though? They all represented the same thing.

Ironically, Sophie's store circularly cements preppy subculture as a new demographic. The term's meaning would never have been distilled this far if it weren't for businesses like hers leaning into trending buzzwords, building demand for their new identities on social media, and then inspiring other businesses to hop on the trend. Sophie tells me that after she started posting as "the preppiest shop in New York City," other stores like dear hannah, prep also rebranded themselves with labels like "the preppiest boutique in Texas." As these companies take cues from each other, they collectively generate a subculture that people buy into.

Meanwhile, the old preparatory school "preppy" was subdivided by social media into new aesthetic microlabels, like "old money," "dark academia," and "light academia," all of which came with their own marketing, their own influencer hauls, and their own TikTok shop tie-ins.* Who cares about old definitions when you can use new labels to create new demand? The real winners, of course, are the social media platforms, which take a commission from all these newly created sales. How convenient for them.

· · · · · · · ·

---

* It's not a coincidence that these all sound like SEO descriptions.

In 2022, the Canadian writer Cory Doctorow coined the term "enshittification" to describe the inevitable decline in quality on all social media platforms. It's a brilliant observation, pointing at their economic priorities at three different points in time:

1. First, social media platforms will make the experience as good as possible for their users, to build up a consistent following.
2. Once users are locked into the app, the platforms will make the experience as good as possible for business customers trying to advertise to that following.
3. Once users *and* businesses are locked in, platforms will exploit both of them to make as much money as possible for their shareholders.[8]

Facebook serves as a classic illustration of this model. When I joined the platform, it was a useful, high-quality medium to virtually connect with people I care about. Then it started running more ads, conveniently tied in to Facebook Marketplace. This change was better for sellers, but I had to tolerate it since I now needed the platform to keep in touch with my friends. Finally, once sellers were also dependent on marketing through Facebook, the platform enshittified itself by running more ads and doubling transaction fees—squeezing more revenue out of both users and businesses. It was able to do this by exploiting its sheer dominance in online communication and user data.[9]

Enshittification can take many different forms. Google and Amazon, for example, are selling more and more advertising space at the top of search results. On social media, however, you consume whatever content is placed in front of you through highly personalized recommendations, so enshittification happens through the algorithm. Facebook used to show your friends' content in chronological order, but then reshuffled it to recommend content that aligns with its business priorities. Even though I go on the app exclusively to see updates from my friends, I must now wade through numerous trending meme pages designed to keep my attention; short-form videos clogging my feed; and, of course, an exhausting morass of advertisements.

In a series of papers in the early 2020s, economic researchers at University College London outlined how social media platforms invariably increase profits by decreasing the quality of information being recommended to their audience. By virtue of their oligopoly, all major short-form video platforms are able to ignore user preferences and monetize their attention. This can take the form of pay-to-play models like on Spotify (where artists can take a 30 percent cut for an algorithmic boost) or X (where the only real way to go viral these days is to have X Premium), or it can be much more subtle: a few more recommendations that you might enjoy less but keep you on the app; or a few more advertisements in your feed. The more space given to advertisers, the less products can compete on their own, which means the app can charge even higher fees. Meanwhile, with regular content, platforms can exploit patterns in your behavior to fill your feed with less organic information that fuels your content addiction.[10]

This is where the hyper-compartmentalization of identity by way of language comes in. The more ways you can be categorized using specific, newly created microlabels, the more ways you can be commodified. Social media knows much more about you than your race, gender, and age (the "old demographics"). They now know your niche preferences, like whether you're goblincore or pastel goth or preppy (the "new demographics"). This enables them to send you ever more targeted content—not necessarily to improve your experience, but rather to improve their own bottom line.

As Glenn McDonald pointed out, algorithms don't actually

need labels like "goblincore" to know that you're a goblincore person; they can tell that by turning your behavior into more convenient strings of numbers and then comparing that with other users' behaviors. As a word, "goblincore" is simply a by-product of surveillance capitalism. Creators and companies desperately trying to reach their audience in a terminally enshittified environment are constantly striving for ever more metadata to get there, which inadvertently ends up giving the algorithm more numbers to work with.

The fact that algorithms are pushing more addicting content means that more addicting language is also proliferating. While Instagram in the 2010s was just a neatly curated timeline of your friends' photos, it's now filled with enshittified, recommended Reels that employ attention-getting words. You might not have gotten a video about "rizz" or "skibidi" at the top of your screen when you had a chronological feed, but now more trend-based content is being spread more quickly, precisely because Instagram has learned what will best retain its audience. Same with a lot of our commercialized language: Words are both created and spread because they align with algorithmic priorities.

Even before personalized recommendations, people were manipulating language in the hopes of getting your attention. The early days of SEO saw a wide variety of "spamdexing" techniques meant to rank websites higher in Google results, such as keyword stuffing, repetition of unrelated phrases, and hidden hyperlinks. Search engines have since gotten smarter, but algorithmic spamdexing lives on. The nine "preppy" hashtags Sophie put in her video speak for themselves, and that comes from a well-meaning small business owner. Everybody's doing this, because everybody wants to sell you something. Our new vocabulary reflects this.

Curiously, even though the commercialization of language has seemingly inundated us with an influx of new words, it might also be paradoxically compressing our lexicon. With algorithms, you want to be specific but not *too* specific. I always tag my videos with the hashtags #etymology, #linguistics, and #language, but I would never use more specific metadata, like #metathesis, even if the main subject of my video is metathesis (an etymological sound change process). That's just far too niche for the algorithm to pick up on.

In the same way, despite all the new metadata being absorbed into our speech, there's a lack of nuance. All the "-cores" are just that: some iteration of an adjective attached to the word "core." If you want to use a more specific term for an aesthetic, you might actually miss out on virality because it doesn't seem as intuitive or in vogue as the more generic language: There's a reason "cottagecore" is more popular than other potential keywords like "bucolic."

In other situations, people are additionally incentivized to use misleading terms simply because they don't want to miss out on the SEO. Even though Sophie acknowledges that #maximalist might've been a more accurate word to describe her product lines, she chose to use #preppy because she knew it'd perform better online. Hence, more precise vocabulary may be supplanted by whatever happens to be trending.

In social psychology, in-groups are thought to be shaped through *optimal distinctiveness,* a phenomenon where we balance our need to belong with our need to be distinct. If we're too individualistic, we find it hard to fit in; too conformist, and we don't feel special about ourselves. As such, we gravitate toward groups and identities that strike a middle ground.

Our new microlabels do that perfectly. There are so many options to choose from that you can feel unique, and yet all the options are playing Mad Libs with the same suffix. If everybody is still a "-core" in the end, then you're not really differentiating yourself too much.

It's counterintuitive, but each new microlabel can indeed limit our linguistic scope and creativity rather than expand it. What appears to be a surplus of new identities may instead encourage us to put ourselves in fixed boxes. A "cottagecore" person may be happy as such because the term seems sufficiently specific to capture their personality, while in the past they might've drawn on a colorful array of other descriptors to explain their aesthetic preferences. A musician may not make music for the sake of making music, and instead might produce songs that fit into their conceptions of whatever microgenre is trending on Spotify or TikTok. Me identifying my style as "goblincore" might distract me from other earth-tones clothing I'd otherwise want to buy. Our new need to label ourselves removes the freedom that comes with a lack of labels.

In his famous aesthetic paper "Categories of Art," the philosophy professor Kendall Walton argues that we perceive art in certain categories, and those categories alter our perception of the art. Each aesthetic category comes with a set of "rules" associated with the label, and we judge media based on how it conforms to those rules.[11] With social media creating more categories, then, are we not creating more rules for ourselves? You can't just be a "goth" anymore, with all the possible interpretations that word could hold. You have to be a "cybergoth" or a "tradgoth" or whatever the latest trend is, each with its own unique set of constraints. Despite having more options than ever, we may see true individuality flattened in favor of what a select group of *others* like, because that's what algorithms do. They don't recommend content for *you;* they recommend content based on others *similar* to you.

Nor do you make your own decisions. Your decisions are now curated for you under the guise of personalization, while in reality they're engineered to make platforms as much money as possible. Your aesthetic preferences, your language, your very *identity*—all handed down to you by the positive feedback loop of social media algorithms.

I'm not saying this to fearmonger. From an etymological standpoint, we absorb commercial words into our vocabulary all the time. "Aspirin," "escalator," and "Kleenex" all started out as brand names that we've normalized as part of our language. Language does, however, reflect culture, and it's important to pay attention to it if we want to understand our culture. Right now, it's telling us that algorithms are tangibly impacting our lifestyles, and we should be clear-eyed about the fact that those algorithms reflect social media's business priorities.

# 9

...........

## OK Boomer

Two hundred years ago, the idea of a "generation" didn't really exist. Sure, the word was around, but mostly in the sense of a *familial* generation—a group of people one step descended from a shared ancestor. The idea of a cultural age cohort—a *social* generation such as the "millennials" or "baby boomers"—did not quite gain traction until the twentieth century, when a confluence of factors created an opportunity for the labels to suddenly make sense. Technological and economic innovations made it possible to live in a more connected way, while shared social experiences like the world wars united people on a truly global level for the first time.

We began with the "Lost Generation," a cultural label to describe the demographic group entering adulthood during World War I, and the "GI Generation," which collectively fought in World War II. Once we started categorizing age groups by common experiences, we couldn't stop. Next came the Silent Generation, the baby boomers, and Gen X, named for a "desire not to be defined" (kick-starting the pattern of naming genera-tions after letters of the alphabet). With each new cohort, the idea of a "generation" became more real and accepted, to a point where it's hard to imagine society without the labels.[1]

Of course, it's all arbitrary. As someone born four years into Gen Z, I relate far more to young millennials than people ten years my junior who are still somehow in my generation. Nev-ertheless, people will often reductively talk about Gen Z as if we were a monolith that shares the same values and ideas, dis-tinct from those of millennials above us or Gen Alpha below us. Not only does this ignore the diversity of backgrounds that exist in any age bracket, but it is also Western-centric: The way we "define" a generation usually relies on a shared experience in the United States above all else. Research has repeatedly failed to identify convincing evidence for the existence of distinct gen-erations, and in 2021 a group of 170 social scientists signed an open letter asking the Pew Research Center to stop using the "misleading" and "pseudoscientific" labels.[2]

These efforts appear to be in vain, especially in recent years. Google Trends shows significantly heightened interest in the phrases "Gen Z," "boomer," and "millennial" starting in the late 2010s, while "Gen Alpha" suddenly sprang onto the scene in the early 2020s. Tens of thousands of articles have been writ-ten about various generational trends, from "millennial pink" and "millennial socks" to the "Gen Z tattoo" and "Gen Z finger heart" (formed with the pointer and middle fingers, instead of the traditional thumb and pointer).

I'm partially guilty of this. I've written op-eds about the lin-guistics behind "Gen Z emojis," and I've used generational labels several times in this book. There is a certain convenience to cat-egories, and as a creator I know it feeds into what people want to see; having gotten to this latter part of the book, you know exactly why that is. At the same time, I'm perpetuating simplistic stereotypes, and I see many other writers and influencers do the same for clicks.

Even though generational labels might be functionally meaningless, their cultural salience appears to have increased in the social media era. People *perceive* generations to be real, to a point where they've developed actual meaning in the popular consciousness, with memes being slung around like new lines of attack in an ongoing intergenerational war. "Boomer" has become an insult in memes like "OK boomer"; Gen Z makes fun of millennials for starting videos with the "millennial pause"; millennials deride the "Gen Z shake."

Part of this perception comes out of inherently different relationships with technology. Unlike older cohorts, most millennials are "digital natives" who grew up with the internet, while most of Gen Z is further distinguished by growing up fully within the context of social media. This likely contributes to Gen Z being frustrated with millennials acting inept online, and both generations feeling frustrated with the out-of-touch boomers.

The different stages of being online also mean that each generation has grown up in a different period of meme history, resulting in a subtle cultural polarization over what we find funny. Boomers, who grew up with newspaper cartoons, are caricatured as enjoying single-panel comics making fun of "the wife" or "kids these days." Millennials, who grew up in the era of image macros, LOLcats, and Advice Animal memes, are thought to try too hard at being "quirky." Gen Z, meanwhile, has become known for their sense of wry yet detached absurdism. Even our emojis are different: Older generations tend to use them literally, while younger generations have increasingly abstracted them to varying degrees of irony. The laughing-crying emoji, for instance, has been successively replaced by the crying emoji and then the skull emoji to indicate humor.

Again, these are broad generalizations. One millennial can have a vastly different sense of humor from another millennial, and some boomers use emojis more adeptly than some Zoomers. Nevertheless, the *stereotypes* really do exist. Even if research tells us there isn't scientific backing to the idea of generations, they exist in our minds much like a zodiac or Myers-Briggs personality: academically meaningless, yet culturally meaningful. In contrast to a hundred years ago, the *idea* of a generation has become an important part of how we talk about our society, and it's been turbocharged by the internet.

In the same way that social media pushes us to identify with commercial identities or niche subgroups, we are further pushed to identify with our generational cohort. Much like preppy subculture or the Swiftie community, "Gen Z" and "millennial" serve as new demographics in the digital information panopticon. Now that they've reinforced the idea that generations exist, platforms have been able to simultaneously drive more personalized recommendations and sell more specific data, which translates to external economic impact—similar to our discussion about microlabels in the previous chapter. People have written entire books about how to "market to Gen Z"; I myself have been invited to speak at "Gen Z marketing" conferences; and there's a long-running joke that the "Gen Z intern" will always make more viral videos through their absurd editing skills.

No programmer was ever told to sit down and make generations hate each other online, and these differences are perhaps less profitable than more commercial microlabels. Nonetheless, generations have emerged as another way for the algorithm to categorize us, and for us to categorize ourselves. As before, this is driven through virality, trends, and filter bubbles. Labels like "millennial pink" not only are trendbait but also help to create in-groups and out-groups by both unifying the Gen Z perspective against millennials and unifying millennials in their own defense. The categorization of demographic time periods like-wise feels similar to the pattern of naming our summers, in that it's all a positive feedback loop: Each additional video compar-ing "Gen Z" with "millennials" reinforces the idea of a category existing. At a certain point, the concept of generations became important simply because it became important, in the same way that the Kardashians became famous simply because they became famous.

........

Even before the idea of social generations, slang drove a wedge of frustration between adults and youths. People typically get upset when the language they grew up with evolves, either because the concept of a "standard language" was ingrained in their educa-tion or because new words make them defensively aware of their own obsolescence.

As such, the increased importance of generations has also brought about a rise of "generational slang," the notion that different age cohorts have their own unique style of speaking. Wikipedia has a compilation of more than a hundred terms in its "List of Generation Z Slang," from incel words like "mew-ing" and "looksmaxxing" to AAE-derived words like "ate," "bet," and "cap." Of course, there's a lot of variation in who uses these words, but what matters here is the *perception* that these words now somehow "belong to Gen Z." This association makes it eas-ier to dismiss language as "slang" (which, if you remember, is an arbitrary construct perpetuating equally arbitrary norms about what language "should" be).

Due to a perfect storm of factors, we're perceiving more "gen-erational slang" than ever before. Wikipedia doesn't have a list of "millennial slang," but it does have a page for "2000s slang," because slang still existed then, but was considered less "generational" in the past.

Since then, social media has changed everything. The breakneck pace of internet trends brings words to the forefront more quickly, while the hard-to-trace nature of meme diffusion allows us to put those words in new conceptual classifications. The way these words reach us online makes them highly obtrusive, so it's easier to identify them as belonging to a generation, while the very idea of "slang" is less isolated to individual groups like the Cockney community or speakers of African American English. Instead, all of it is subsumed into this new idea of a generational lexicon. Etymology is forgotten and each word further contributes to generational friction.

The best example of this is the term "brainrot," used to describe the class of "internet slang words" commonly associated with Gen Alpha. In the early 2020s, this especially included the kind of language found in the Rizzler song: so-called cringe vocabulary like "rizz," "gyat," "skibidi," "fanum tax," and "sigma" that we encountered in chapter 2. Although these words were actually used by millions of middle-schoolers, the perception that they "belong to Gen Alpha" is naturally a gross generalization. Each term came from a niche older source and experienced a range of usage across generational boundaries.

The difference, however, was what "brainrot" represented. As a concept, the label covered both the subset of "Gen Alpha vocabulary" and the idea that that vocabulary "rotted the brain"—that it was somehow indicative of their unhealthy online presence.[*]

This, of course, is untrue. There's no evidence that internet slang is ruining our writing or composition abilities. The impact of the internet as a whole on child development is another

---

[*] This notion so profoundly impacted our relationship with the internet that the Oxford University Press chose "brain rot" as its 2024 Word of the Year.

conversation to have, but as a linguist I find myself always having to emphasize that there's nothing remotely harmful about the *words* we categorize as "brainrot."

"Skibidi," for instance, has often been touted as an indicator of how the youth is being corrupted, but it's etymologically no different from the name Scooby-Doo: Both were nonsense words created from scat singing that were later reapplied to fictional cartoon characters, and yet "skibidi" is considered brainrot while "Scooby-Doo" is normal.

In the same way, there's never anything inherently harmful about the newness of any word. The reality is that kids always develop slang to build identity. Having their own language gives them a sense of community that they can't have with adults, but because the adults are excluded, they always criticize those kids for "corrupting" the English language. Eventually, the kids grow up, their language is normalized, and the cycle continues on mercilessly.

The newly generational associations behind "brainrot," however, made it easier than ever to voice those criticisms. Suddenly it wasn't just about Gen Alpha corrupting language; it was about Gen Alpha corrupting their own *minds* with deleterious vocabulary. Beyond stigmatizing a normal etymological process, this directly harms other communities: Consider what happens to the in-groups that came up with those slang words, like the AAE speakers who came up with "gyat." Their language suddenly becomes marked with a toxic generational label. The word becomes obtrusive, and (as you might remember from chapter 2) obtrusive words tend to die out.

In 2023, *The New York Times* published an article titled "Gen Alpha Is Here. Can You Understand Their Slang?" In it, the author specifically uses "sigma," "rizz," and "gyat" as examples of how "social media really exacerbates" generational differences, and interviews a middle-schooler named Jaedyn about her usage of the words. "If millennials start saying them," she says, "we'll be like, 'We're done with these now.'"[3]

There's so much to unpack here. Jaedyn's quotation shows how niche words that are brought to the mainstream eventually get discarded, but it also shows how that's accelerated through her identification against a generational label (which would not have been a thing a hundred years ago). Even the *Times* gives credibility to the idea of "generational slang" in its title, lending its journalistic ethos to the concept. In reality, it played into the idea because a confusing out-group is guaranteed to draw in readers (which is also why "Gen Alpha" is overused on social media: It draws in viewers). Each additional article like this further reinforces the notion, to the point where our very curiosity manifests its existence.

If no one ever paid attention to the Rizzler song in October 2023, none of its words would have become "brainrot," but people *were* interested in it, since it was a "Gen Alpha" meme. That made the song trend, so it really *did* go viral among Gen Alpha, so there was even more reason to fixate on generational slang. The way we dramatize everything online created a positive feedback loop of real generational tribalism, which continues driving itself.

· · · · · · · ·

In the television entertainment industry, screenwriters have to be constantly wary about *Flanderization,* or accidentally simplifying their characters through the exaggeration of certain personality quirks. The eponymous example is Ned Flanders from *The Simpsons,* who slowly evolves from a well-meaning religious neighbor to a Christian fundamentalist throughout the course of the series. Over time, the commercially popular aspects of the character were enhanced to appeal to the show's fan base, but it actually worked against the show by making Ned Flanders feel shallower.

Beyond TV writing, Flanderization is alive and well on social media. Creators regularly caricature themselves for the sake of more views, because we have to stay relevant. I've watched many a TikTok series where an influencer plays a funny persona, but then hyperbolizes that persona as they try to optimize for more engagement or to maintain interest. I've even felt a dissonance over doing this with my own online presence: My "Etymology Nerd" brand started out as me talking about words I like, but eventually evolved into a caricature of my passion for linguistics. I still like what I'm talking about, but I deliver it in a manic, excited style that I know people will prefer to watch.

I'd even argue that Flanderization is *more* pronounced on social media. While screenwriters exaggerate their characters in response to years of Nielsen ratings and fan input, influencers must respond to algorithmic pressures on a much shorter timeline, since they're churning out a faster pace of content in a faster-paced environment. We're already incentivized to present a cohesive brand image and to lean into what performs well, which means that we'll inevitably typecast ourselves.

This is easily observable in speech patterns like the influencer accents, but now consider word choice. Some words clearly generate more engagement than other words, so of course we'll trend toward reusing successful language. If saying "Gen Z" gets more views and clicks than the phrases "young people" or "2000s kids," then we're going to talk about Gen Z more; that's just the way it works. Of course, that makes "Gen Z" even more successful as a label, so more people will use it, unknowingly optimizing for oversimplified vocabulary.

Consider, too, *why* so much of our slang eventually gets labeled as brainrot. Creators use words whenever they're trending, but at a certain point these words get cycled through the engagement treadmill so many times that they feel overused and meaningless. Previously unique terms are reduced until they're thought of as more mind-numbing additions to our oversaturated slang lexicon. Language becomes a parody of itself, deriving absurdity from its algorithmic origins. Then we question it all: How could "Gen Alpha" possibly come up with such stupid vocabulary?

This is where we get into the Flanderization of subcultures. If creators know that concise narrative-driven labels feel more compelling or are more likely to go viral, we'll exaggerate our own identities and play a real part in shaping the cultural conversation, the same way "preppy" emerged from a Flanderization of the popular-girl aesthetic.

Flanderization of identity isn't new—some observers have argued that the beatniks simplified the true philosophy of the Beat writers—but it's absolutely happening faster because of the internet. Since an over-the-top exaggerated video of a "tradwife" living a hyper-cottagecore lifestyle is going to perform better than a tangentially cottagecore video, that will inform our idea of what "cottagecore" really means. Then, when people consume and identify with cottagecore content, they identify closer with the extreme idea that was presented to them. Even if a creator isn't *intentionally* exaggerating their videos, we know that social media will still amplify more extreme perspectives by virtue of their attention-grabbing ability, inadvertently normalizing those perspectives in our subcultures.

The danger, of course, is that we consign our own identities to extreme versions of themselves. The more I see the label "Gen Z" used on social media, the more I resonate with the concept of being Gen Z myself, and the more I internalize the cultural expectations we place on being Gen Z. That could mean buying into little actions like using the "Gen Z finger heart" or consciously filming videos with the "Gen Z shake"—both very overgeneralized attributes for people my age—but it's also a bigger thing since it's a part of how I categorize myself as a person. If that categorization is Flanderized with time, perhaps my identity is as well.

The simplification of labels into reductive categories like "Gen Z" and "millennial" additionally makes it easier to reduce age into an us-versus-them binary, leading into intergenerational tribalism. The more we believe these differences exist, the easier it is to think negatively about them, and make those differences feel real. Every "OK boomer" and every complaint about "Gen Alpha brainrot" feeds into the cycle and realizes it.

In 2023, researchers at the Kellogg School of Management found that the way algorithms filter content has fundamentally changed how we engage in social learning. We've always acquired new behaviors by mimicking the actions of others, but algorithms bring us content representing the most extreme behaviors of others. Again, this leads to us thinking that the extreme is more normal than it is. People are increasingly overestimating how far their views are from the other side of the political spectrum, and how distinct their identities are from others. Because a lot of social learning occurs subconsciously through imitation, we're also starting to imitate these extreme representations, which might be how certain "generational behaviors" became so popular in the first place. Our brains have been hijacked into identifying with Flanderizations.[4]

........

Generations are a convenient microcosm of internet communities, showing how social media divisionism can increase the importance of recently manufactured labels. Like any communities, however, our generations are more than mere labels to us:

They represent the *stories* we can tell about ourselves and the types of people we are.

Beyond stereotypes or oversimplifications, we build these stories through a shared canon of references. Each stereotype we *do* create for ourselves, from the idea that Gen Z makes a different finger heart to the idea that we shake our phones before filming, actually started as a reference to some video or article where that difference was first identified. Calling back to it is an act of drawing on our shared canon, akin to how a history teacher might quote Shakespeare or your grandmother might quote a cultural proverb. You assume that the person you're talking to will understand that reference due to the shared culture between you.

It's the gestalt of these little shared things that make up identity. A *Merriam-Webster* definition doesn't make me "Gen Z," but I can be won over to the label by connecting my experiences to the many associations of what "Gen Z" encompasses. Once I cross a certain tipping point, I'll actively seek ways to adopt differences like the "Gen Z heart" to align my perceived and actual identities—accepting outside stories and characteristics to explain who I am.

Identities have always been constructed out of stories. The American national identity is built on foundational myths such as George Washington's cherry tree and Paul Bunyan; on real stories like the Declaration of Independence and the War of 1812; and on shared literature like the Pledge of Allegiance or the works of Washington Irving. Without all of these references, my "American" nationality would have no significance to me; but I grew up in the context of these stories, so I can tie them into my idea of what it means to be American.

The same thing is happening on social media, and not just with generational identity—with all subcommunities. Each additional post is a contribution to the common folklore of the filter bubble it belongs to. Influential videos get stitched, reposted, and referred to in the comments sections of other videos, automatically recommended through hyperlinks or pre-filled-in search bars. To be caught up on these references is to belong in the in-group.

Meme culture especially provides frameworks and shared references by drawing on preexisting templates, inherently alluding back to common pieces of culture. I'm particularly drawn to one mega-viral 2024 video from a plastic surgeon, captioned "I hired a Gen Z editor and this is what they sent me." In the video, the substance of the surgeon's message is entirely cut out so that all we hear is every time he takes a breath. It's a funny joke, but only because it draws on so many existing tropes: the recurring idea of the "Gen Z intern" making funny edits, the recurring idea of a technological split between generations, and the recurring idea of older people breathing heavily.

Indeed, this is reflected in the video's top comment, which says "gen x breath / millennial pause / gen z shake / whats next 🙀 🙏" with bright blue links highlighting all the perceived generational trends. If you were to click on those links, they would take you to the TikTok search page, where you could watch more videos about each of those perceived social differences. Both the original comment and the video refer back subtly to existing generational discourse, since they only make sense in light of it.

Social media does this as a whole, and each app is a sub-culture in its own right. Anybody spending time on TikTok in the early 2020s would see viral videos analogized to the Bella Poarch head-bopping video, visual edits compared to the "salt transition," and their For You page torn over app-wide dramas that held no relevance in the real world. Few online references ever do; they instead serve to affirm the social media folklore that defines the culture of being online. Social media companies, of course, benefit from these references, since they help you identify as a user of their platforms. Beyond that, each hyper-linked reference is good for TikTok or YouTube simply because it draws you into the rabbit hole long enough to forget why you were there in the first place.

Occasionally, online intertextuality escapes cyberspace and becomes used in real life. "Roman Empire" and "girl dinner" both became widely used phrases offline, even though they originally called back to specific videos. This isn't new. Look at all the quotations we borrowed from Shakespeare: "Brevity is the soul of wit"; "To thine own self be true." When these expressions are said in real life, we no longer think about how they came from *Hamlet,* just like how the people saying "Roman Empire" didn't really think back to the original video when they used the phrase. Nevertheless, our language gets built out of these shared cultural references. Media always shapes culture.

This is why so many algospeak euphemisms are specific to the online domain of use. Words like "sewerslide" and "seggs" are understood as shared vernacular in the algospace. To use them is to recognize that they are pieces of the social media sociolect and culture. The "brainrot" genre, especially, relies on shared folklore. Each word is only funny when it refers back to the running history of other brainrot words. Memes are neces-sarily understood in the context of other memes; terms like "ski-bidi" are popularized as post-ironic nods to the very culture that spawned the overuse of niche comedic references.

Of course, many more references remain out of reach, due to the simple fact that you can't ever know every reference at once. Shakespeare scholars will always be able to quote his more obscure verses, while avid social media users will always be able to reference more niche videos. These only matter if you're already deep into the in-group. Interestingly, that's precisely *when* they matter: when they help to contextualize our shared identities.

Academics often speak about folklore in a separate context from linguistics, and as separate from media studies, but the truth is that they're all constantly meshing. By its own nature, our language is self-referential. Our words call back to our media; our media fits into our interdiscursive web of stories; and our stories in turn produce more words.

This raises an interesting corollary: Since social media is building more communities with more internal references, our folkloric language is developing faster than ever before. Each community comes with its own canon of stories, and when an idea is compelling outside that canon, it slips through to the mainstream. Meanwhile, within the in-groups, memes allow cultures to define themselves around shared folklore. This can nuance the cultures by deepening the meanings behind their identities, but it can also Flanderize them by constraining them to the oversimplified narratives they've built up. The meaning of "Gen Z" implies far more than it once did because of memes like the "Gen Z intern," but it's also been reduced. Meanings create boxes, and we put ourselves into those boxes every time we believe stories about who we are.

Curiously, the rise of internet folklore is reflected in our vocabulary through the word "lore," which has increased four-fold in Google search interest over the past two decades. You'll often hear younger people talk about their own pasts as "lore," or even extend it to any mundane context; under my video for the etymology of "apricot," a top comment says, "Apricot lore is crazy." It's as if our language were reflexively aware of its own narrative building.

. . . . . . . .

Stories and definitions are unavoidable. In fact, they're a fundamental part of what makes us human. The consensus in evolutionary neuroscience is that we evolved pattern recognition and episodic memory as survival mechanisms, since they're necessary for crucial behaviors like learning and socializing. Once we were able to tie causes to events, we were better suited for reacting to stimuli in our environment.

We also turned into meaning-making machines, unable to shake ourselves from thinking in discrete categories. This is why we keep making in-groups and out-groups and why we change our identities to fit perceptual categories. Any of these distinctions are, of course, completely meaningless outside our cognition, but the story feels good to us because we crave identifiable patterns over random noise.

What we choose to categorize is, of course, a reflection of our technological and cultural environment. When everybody was walking around in togas and tunics, there was no need to distinguish goths and punks, but now that fashion and social media have created more options, we can even distinguish between pastel goths and vampire goths. While the idea of "generations" didn't make much sense in the past, our increased connectivity made the categories more useful, even if they are simplistic generalizations.

Not only are our categories shaped by our technology, but the stories we build around them are, too. Prior to written history, stories in the oral tradition were often preserved through song, for it was easier for people to remember ideas when they had rhyme and meter. Once we transitioned to manuscripts, we were able to introduce more varied literary styles and segment our stories into chapters.

Algorithms have once again changed the way we tell stories. Exaggerated, attention-grabbing rhetorical devices are as important in the online medium as song was in ancient Greece. Beyond that, the *structure* of our stories has gotten simpler in short-form video. It's hard to get a detailed point across within the constraint of a minute, and too much nuance can be confusing to viewers when you're trying to retain their attention. This means that creators have largely eschewed complexity in favor of virality.

I often feel frustrated that my videos only perform well when I push a single angle to my story. Etymology is often a messy thing that can't be neatly packaged into linear explanations; sometimes words aren't related but still influence each other, and other times origins are uncertain. Nevertheless, my videos will only go viral if I present things through cohesive, confident narratives. The trial-and-error process has repeatedly taught me that simple stories do better numbers than complex ones.

The human brain really likes simplicity, and algorithms appeal to the brain's subconscious desires, so naturally the algorithm will push stories and categories that feel satisfyingly simple to us. Readily understandable labels and explanations are not only easier to consume; they feel *better* to consume.

By itself, that's pretty normal. We also like it when books make sense. Most of us would rather read *Harry Potter* than *Ulysses* because the former is more accessible. The difference is that while a *Harry Potter*-type miniseries could be possible to replicate on social media, *Ulysses* would never have succeeded on TikTok. It's too disjointed, too nonlinear, requires too much conscious attention. People would scroll away.

So we use more overt, simple narratives online. Indeed, a lot of our newer slang shows a trend toward simplified storytelling in our everyday lives. Beyond the word "lore," younger people will often talk about themselves as if they were the "main characters" in some kind of show. We do things "for the plot"; we go through "canon events"; we have "character arcs" and "eras." Deviations from the storyline are written off as "side-quests," while tangential characters in our lives are dismissed as "NPCs." People have always talked like this to some extent—

describing "chapters" in the "story" of our lives—but there's a greater sense of a structure than perhaps ever before.

All of these metaphors spread on social media through people making narratives out of their lives. Because their brand depends on personal connection, the only way for lifestyle influencers to go viral is to tell stories about themselves. A makeup video won't do well by itself, but a "get ready with me" video where the influencer tells a story while applying makeup will. We've never had such regular, intimate access into the lives of media personalities, but now we constantly consume "storytime" videos where this style of narrative language is frequently used. We're exposed to narrative-building words so much that it's no wonder we're starting to use them more frequently offline.

The storytelling phenomenon is present well beyond my style of educational content or the lifestyle influencer's style of personal content. In gaming and meme communities, the discourse marker "POV" frequently precedes video captions, inviting you to experience a story firsthand. Regular gaming clips don't do as well anymore; they now have to be presented through a more interactive lens. No corner of the internet succeeds without simplifying content into stories.

These reductive stories are interchangeable with reductive categories. "Categories" are just stories we tell ourselves about how we're similar to or different from each other, and these stories become even simpler through self-Flanderization. It feels so much easier to frame age differences as generational, so we reduce our identities to fit those labels. It's easier to talk about your fashion preferences when you're a pastel goth instead of a catchall goth, so you microlabel yourself, even if that removes the freedom of the broader label.

These categories, in turn, play an inextricable part in defining our self-image. Each time we create or adopt a new category, we tell ourselves a story that helps us frame our identity in relation to it. A good analogy is the queer community, which jokingly calls itself the alphabet mafia for its overabundance of micro-labels. In addition to the traditional LGBTQIA+ identities, there are dozens of sexual orientations and "xenogenders" entirely new to the internet era. However, many in the community have grown frustrated with these terms, since a lot of queer identity has traditionally been about rejecting labels. Gender and sexuality can be very fluid, and prescribing categories can not only limit that fluidity but also project contemporary Western frameworks onto identity. The same problem is true with any label: It constrains true self-expression into boxes, each of which comes with its own semantic baggage.

Our blind trust in algorithms helps us believe in the categories assigned to us. Even though personalized recommendations are *probabilistic*—trying to predict what we like—we often treat them as *deterministic,* as if they already *know* what we like. Through that attitude, we become "calcified in our digital identities," each of which can be uniquely tagged and marketed to.[5]

On some level, most of us know this. Nevertheless, it's incredibly tempting and easy to mold ourselves to labels. The greater breadth of folklore attached to each category makes it feel more real, with more natural ways to identify with it. The amount of storytelling we're exposed to makes it easier to perceive our own identities as fitting into neat stories. "Gen Z," "millennial," and "boomer" are just that—stories more than descriptions, about the type of person we are based on the age cohort we were born into. Each comes with its own intricate web of lore and memes, and they're so beautifully convenient!

As a result, we accept these stories, spread them on social media, and begin to conceptualize our own identities as fitting into those narratives. Internally, we might feel as though the narratives help us categorize our individuality, but on paper they all rely on the same stories. It doesn't matter how much I label myself: If I'm a demisexual goblincore Gen Z Swiftie, I guarantee there are still others like me. The only thing those labels really change about me is that they make me easier to classify and market to. Ironically, true individuality may come out of a *lack* of labels and stories, because there's greater freedom of expression with a blank slate. If everybody's the "main character," then nobody is.

## 10

...........

# Are We Cooked?

Y OU'RE TEACHING SPANISH in a classroom in Chile, and you're confused. Your students keep using all these new slang words, and it's nearly impossible to keep up. *Si quieres ser un sigma,* one tells you, *deberías hacer el mewing.* "If you want to be a sigma, you should do the mewing." Then he high-fives his classmate because his joke *low-key devoró,* or "low-key ate." Meanwhile, the popular kids compliment one another's outfits, and you hear: *Eslei. Estás sirviendo.* "Slay. You're serving."

The scenario is fictitious, but the words are real. I've surveyed Chilean teachers who hear this kind of language every day in school, and I've seen dozens of Spanish-language TikToks replicating, word for word, the social media slang I've written about in this book. Sometimes kids will directly adopt loanwords, like "delulu" (which was borrowed without change), and sometimes they'll calque it into their own language, like turning "unalive" into *desvivir* (analogizing *vivir* to "alive"). The same is true for virtually every language: In Portuguese, you can *fazer o mewing,* while in Arabic you can practice الميوويينق (another transliteration of "mewing").

Never before has slang been so global. Words would occasionally slip from one language to another, but now every successful trend immediately gets replicated online in the span of a few days, enabling "social media language" to become universal. Of course, with each translation, context continues to get lost, like the fact that *devoró* comes from the New York drag community or that *el mewing* was popularized by incel circles. Nevertheless, social media is highly connective, ensuring that our words, memes, and SEO terms will inevitably spread.

This global spread also demonstrates the increased impact of the English language. Before the internet, English had already accrued significant cultural capital from being the dominant language in trade and international relations, but it was still more separate from the informal language used in people's daily lives. This distinction was enforced by language planning institutes such as the Real Academia Española (RAE) in Madrid and the Académie Française in Paris, respectively tasked with monitoring and standardizing the Spanish and French languages. Whenever a word needed to be translated, media outlets would turn to them as the official arbiters of "correct" Spanish or French. Thus, these academies could subtly shape culture by enforcing "Spanish-sounding" or "French-sounding" calques over direct loanwords, which were thought of as "corruptive." Just as with the idea of "standard English," these norms propagated a single upper-class dialect as the proper version of language. Unlike English, they were given direct institutional backing, meaning that the language evolved in a more standard, centralized direction.

The internet, particularly through social media, has changed everything. English is indisputably the lingua franca online.

More than half of all the internet is written in it, and non-native speakers from different countries will almost always default to English to communicate with each other. Trends in other languages follow trends in English, and the same goes with specific words. Media is no longer beholden to institutional gatekeeping and verification; nowadays, anyone can post anything anytime. This is taking power out of the hands of traditional censors and kick-starting a newly decentralized era in etymology.

Of the sixty-nine Spanish-language teachers I surveyed, many were quick to note that *desvivir* already had an RAE-sanctioned definition of "do your utmost," but that their kids weren't using the word this way. Instead, they were using it for the same reasons that Americans say it: either to avoid algorithmic censorship, or as a genuine euphemism for "commit suicide." The kids don't care about the language academy's thoughts on the matter, and the language academy can't do much about it anyway. Spanish is evolving much more by itself, untethered from arbitrary norms that previously held it down.

The same thing is happening in French, where the Académie Française is losing its grip on a language disproportionately spoken outside France. Young Africans in former French colonies, increasingly disconnected from the imposed "standard" version of their language, are innovating on social media by incorporating more Arabic loanwords into their self-expression. Much to the chagrin of the Académie, these are becoming popular well outside Africa: Terms like *cheh* (serves you right) and *wesh* (what's up) have become mainstream throughout France due to their increased presence in social media and rap lyrics. Music and memes, especially, draw on language as it's actually spoken; this is because it simply feels more natural. And as media starts trending, the words spread faster in a pattern that should now be all too familiar to us.[1]

Even within English, the rapid growth of "slang" reflects a

shift away from language being controlled by elites. Although it's still an uphill battle, people have started to normalize speaking in "nonstandard" dialects like African American English. The nature of user-generated content means that anyone can have a platform, removing agency from the prescriptive powers that be and kick-starting an entirely new decolonization of language.

Even where it appears as if governments were doing a good job of asserting control, new language always slips through the cracks. Despite prolific censorship in China, for example, social media users have easily been able to sneak through clever algospeak substitutions. When the word for "censorship" began to be censored in the early twenty-first century, people pivoted to use the word *héxié,* meaning "harmonious" in an ironic reference to the CCP's goal of building a "harmonious society." Then, once *héxié* also began to be censored, users switched to the homophone *héxiè,* which technically meant "river crab" but was understood as standing in for "harmonious." At a certain point, other users also started using *shuǐchǎn,* a phrase meaning "aquatic product," in substitution of "river crab." Hundreds of similar replacements exist for various words, making it incredibly difficult for the government to regulate every single change.[2]

In fact, research suggests that it's impossible for censors to win the Whac-A-Mole game. A 2015 Georgia Tech study found that it was so easy to replace sensitive Chinese keywords with understandable homophones that if every potential homophone were flagged on social media, 20 percent of all posts would be taken down as false positives—rendering the websites unusable.[3] That's just from moving around tones, ignoring potential semantic substitutions, so we're clearly quite far from a *1984*-esque scenario. Large language models may get better at recognizing words in context, but people will always find creative ways to express their ideas.

We've already seen this in action. During the 2019 Hong

Kong protests, antigovernment social media users took to writing out messages in "Kongish," a blend of Cantonese and English romanized to disguise their communication from Chinese-language algorithms. To make their code even harder to crack, the protesters replaced sensitive keywords with evasive euphemisms: "ghost" for "undercover cop," "rain" for "pepper spray," and "shopping" for "attending a protest." These worked particularly well; imagine how challenging it must be to censor the words "rain" or "shopping" online.

The Kongish writing style was notably playful and meme based. One image, covered in cartoon characters, advises what to do "if u wai yi yau ghost" (if you suspect there might be an undercover cop). The writing is tongue-in-cheek, ignoring romanization conventions the same way "unalive" and *desvivir* emerged as childish yet effective ways to talk about a censored topic. Throughout the protest, sentences like this one diffused within the protester in-group as memes, simultaneously defying the Chinese government and building community online.[4]

Centralized social media platforms might seem nominally easy to control, but we've clearly shown ourselves to be quite ingenious at algospeak. Mass communication has been put into the hands of everyday citizens, meaning that language can do its own thing, unfettered from government inhibition.

. . . . . . . .

"Sigmas of Australia," begins Senator Fatima Payman in a September 2022 speech to the Australian parliament. "I say that this goofy ahh government have been capping. Not just now, but for a long time. A few of you may remember when they said 'there will be no Fanum Tax under a government I lead.'" In her viral video, Senator Payman goes on to urge people to vote so that they can "mog" her "opps" in the government.

Payman's remarks are strikingly reminiscent of another speech, by the Canadian senator Bernadette Clement in May of the same year. "Honorable fam, waiting to vote until 18 is a big yikes," she says. "Today's youth slays and stays bussin."

Senators Payman and Clement were clearly using these words for their shock value, but their speeches showcase the growing influence of online language in the offline world. These politicians were only able to craft these speeches using the sheer amount of new, culturally salient slang available to us. They then used that slang as an attention-getting tactic, exactly the same way that many creators use it online.

"Sigmas of Australia" might not be the new "Friends, Romans, countrymen," but it shows how even our governmental institutions must now adapt to the algorithm if they want to stay relevant. Politicians are incentivized to conduct at least part of their campaigns through social media, meaning that their public communication becomes subordinated to algorithmic pressures. What this portends is that our campaigning and political discourse will increasingly be shaped by what goes viral.

This is also true of media outlets. Young people are overwhelmingly turning to sources like TikTok and Instagram for their news, so traditional media outlets have had to work within those conduits. In many cases, these accounts are run by older, less media-savvy people: Looking at the *New York Times* and *Wall Street Journal* profiles, they both regularly release videos with far fewer views than my minimum view count. Having personally interacted with the media divisions of multiple major news outlets, I can tell you it's not for a lack of quality reporting. It's because these news sources are run by journalists first and social media creators second.

Now contrast that with Dylan Page, the self-proclaimed News Daddy of TikTok, broadcasting to tens of millions of followers. Every single one of his videos receives millions of views with much higher engagement than those of the traditional outlets, simply because he knows how to play the algorithmic game. His videos open with bright colors, bold claims, and a recognizable influencer accent. Dylan is a social media creator first, journalist second, and it shows. Though he's likely making a positive impact overall, he often ends up sensationalizing or reducing his stories to appeal to his audience. The *Journal* and *Times* don't do this, which is why their views languish in the tens of thousands.

Of course, it's hard to verify what is and isn't good journalism online, and that uncertainty has led to a rise in misinformation online. Sometimes, it's unintentional: Creators might leave out the whole picture or incorrectly reinterpret a source despite their best intentions. Even with thorough research, I've made numerous mistakes in my videos because they aren't passing through a secondary editorial process. In other instances, however, people spread intentional and malicious disinformation: Deepfakes, hoaxes, and conspiracy theories have proliferated online out of various attempts to sway politics or public opinion.

At the same time, algorithms aren't all bad. In democratizing public communication, they've given us more access than ever to public video evidence and records, making it harder for governments to do bad things. Now that anybody can have a platform, it's harder for elite powers to set the agenda by manufacturing consent through traditional media. I believe that there's absolutely something equalizing about the fact that everything is run through the algorithm.

No sector of public communication can escape. Musicians are crafting their songs around shorter and shorter sound bites that are more likely to go viral as trending social media audios, but that also means that anybody with talent and social media savvy can earn an audience. Hollywood is adapting *Skibidi Toilet* into a full-budget film and TV series, suggesting that online content can indeed become a commercially serious thing. Corporations are incorporating popular slang and memes into their advertising; this is necessary if they want to stay relevant in the fast-paced, every-man-for-himself battle for online attention.

The public isn't ignorant of these changes. Younger people, growing up bombarded with ads, distrust marketing more than ever before. We live with the algorithm, but resistance to it is embedded into our counterculture. Our memes grow more self-referential and satirical as inherent reactions against our technological reality. Whether it's "corecore" pushing back against heightened consumerism, or "cringe content" poking fun at the oversaturation of "brainrot" vocabulary, we can tell when something feels unnatural, and we will react against it.

· · · · · · · ·

It can be tough to tell who wins and who loses in the algorithmic era of language change; so much of what's happening on social media is deeply paradoxical. Our personal communication is more regulated than ever, but we also have more ways to evade those regulations. Nonstandard language is more broadly used than ever before, but its presence is constantly perceived and stigmatized. Words are emerging faster and fading faster.

The biggest paradox is how this impacts linguistic diversity. Even the largest video platform, YouTube, supports only 80 languages, despite there being around 7,000 languages worldwide. This is a problem with the internet in general—Google supports only 240 languages and Wikipedia 345 languages—but the issue is amplified on social media, since it only makes sense for the apps to cater to larger audiences where they can create trends and in-groups.

The lack of online resources for languages spoken by smaller populations only contributes to their looming extinction. The consensus is that nearly half of all languages will disappear by the end of the century, with one dying out every other week.[5] This usually happens when speakers shift to more influential languages, and we know social media is making the big languages more influential than ever. There's a great deal of social pressure to communicate in a way you can use online, so it does make sense that social media would be causing some languages to fade away faster.

However, it's unclear how much social media is actually *causing* these languages to decline, versus simply accelerating an existing trend. The linguistic map has always had a complicated history of ebb and flow—this is perfectly natural. We're no longer speaking Etruscan or Sumerian or Common Brittonic, since new languages eventually came along to replace them. In the same way, globalization and increased national identity were already causing the more robust languages to outcompete the lesser-used languages well before the internet came along.

If anything, the internet is playing an important part in documenting and preserving dying languages through initiatives like Wikitongues and the Endangered Languages Project, which are better able to catalog information thanks to modern technology. Language revitalization servers on Discord are bringing together groups of people who are enthusiastic about preserving those languages. In other cases, social media is directly contributing to linguistic diversity by normalizing language variants like Spanglish, which is more represented online than it ever was in older media.

There certainly is a heavy Western bias to languages that *are* available on social media. Even though 7.5 percent of the world's population speaks Hindi, less than 0.1 percent of all websites are in Hindi, while a language like German punches far above its weight (5.5 percent of the internet compared with about 1 percent of global speakers). This means that any social-media-fueled linguicide will disproportionately impact the culture of already marginalized communities.

English, specifically, benefits as the majority language of the internet. It's the same "preferential attachment" process that makes trending memes even trendier: People will latch onto socially desirable languages, making them more widely used, which then makes them more socially desirable. That's why, regardless of any geopolitical shifts, we will likely see English continue to determine global linguistic trends for the foreseeable future across cultures.

At the same time, there's another paradox within English: Many of its regional dialects are dying out. Speakers of British English are trending toward the southern London dialect in lieu of their regional accents for the same reason that Sara Deshmukh felt as if she had to mask her native Indian accent: London English is seen as more prestigious, and more represented, online.[6] Similarly, researchers at the University of Texas at Austin have identified a 60 percent decline in the Texas accent from 1980 to 2013, and the pattern is likely to continue as Standard American English continues to be the prestige dialect on social media.[7] As with the pattern of world languages, though, this process was probably already in place and is just being amplified online. Commenters had already been identifying a "neutralization" or "Midwesternization" of the American accent throughout the greater part of the twentieth century, so I would argue that we aren't experiencing anything particularly new.

This gets even more complicated when we consider that some dialects are becoming *more* prominent online. The Valley girl accent has not only gotten more popular but also spawned numerous offshoots through the new variations of the influencer accent. Interestingly, it's as if linguistic diversity offline were being replaced with linguistic diversity online.

This is especially true if you think about all the specialized dialects being created by online filter bubbles. The Texas and Liverpool dialects may be dying out, but now we have a Swiftie dialect, a K-pop dialect, an incel dialect, a furry dialect, and many others. The change isn't so much about the *disappearance* of dialects as about their *replacement* from a geographic medium to a digital one. Yes, there is a general trend toward Standard American and British English, but it's complemented by the diversity of subcultures on social media.

Historically, linguists have employed the rule of thumb that "the longer a place is settled, the more dialects will form." In traditional geographic settings, it meant that individual towns, social groups, and regions will develop their own linguistic quirks to suit their particular needs, but the maxim can also be applied to the internet. As we're spending more time on social media, we're forming more and more niche communities, which ultimately give us even more dialects. Some of us are even developing multiple accents as we code-switch between the online and the offline contexts, just as people have code-switched throughout time. Regardless of whether any of that helps big tech companies, we're playing out a millennia-old human trend.

In short, the paradox of linguistic diversity is the same as it's always been. Language, now as in the past, is simultaneously converging and diverging; there will always be people trying to identify with and against various in-groups. Accents and dialects are conditioned social responses to those groups, and we will reach a homeostasis of dialectal diversity to match the depth of human diversity.

........

In 2022, *The New York Times* reported that American Sign Language (ASL) was rapidly changing to adapt to the structure of social media. The word for "dog," for example, is traditionally made by tapping one hand onto your waist, but that specific gesture doesn't make as much sense in the age of vertical video, where it would appear off-screen. Instead, social media users have taken to signing the letters *DG* twice, which also looks as if you were snapping for a dog's attention. Although this confuses some older members of the Deaf community, younger members have adapted to their environment by modifying their communication accordingly.

Just as with spoken language, smartphones have also revolutionized ASL. Since you often need to hold your camera with one hand while you communicate with the other, many Deaf people have adapted to make signs with one hand even when they're typically made with both. Since screens and cameras are tighter than in-person communication, many children have learned to sign within a tighter space than their parents. The *Times* points out that this is all popularized through social media, where platforms are both "encouraging tighter gestures and giving the new versions a way to spread quickly."[8]

The Deaf community is particularly susceptible to picking up social media slang, since 90 percent of Deaf children have hearing parents and everyone is already so geographically dispersed. The internet might just be the best way for signers to connect with their community—meaning they are especially responsive to online linguistic changes.

This is totally fine by itself, but it can turn into a problem when the algorithm disproportionately rewards non-Deaf ASL creators. Jon Urquhart, a child of Deaf adults (CODA) with more than 600,000 TikTok followers, explains to me that CODAs and other hearing signers have an automatic advantage online. Most users will scroll away from silent videos, which means the algorithm "rarely pushes videos by Deaf people without English captions or voice-over."

Deaf creators also have more difficulty capitalizing on trending audios, while hearing ASL creators have created a fad out of signing over popular music. So many of these signs are exaggerated or inaccurate that the National Association of the Deaf has had to warn about "devastating harm" from ASL TikTok gibberish. Just as with African American English, the structure of social media pushed minority language into a trend, and our mainstream fascination diluted its original importance.[9] Jon tells me that "hearing people will try and pinpoint" funny-seeming ASL signs and then misuse them.

ASL is the perfect case study for how social media is changing language, since we can literally *see* it happening in front of us. These are physical gestures evolving due to physical constraints, but the same thing also happens when the constraints are less apparent. Invisible, algorithmic rules play as instrumental a role in shaping words as screen size does in shaping signed communication.

The idea that we *can't* see what's happening is naturally a little scary. In his 2024 book, *Filterworld,* the *New Yorker* writer Kyle Chayka identifies "algorithmic anxiety," or a perceived lack of control online, as an outgrowth of our general uncertainty and mistrust about how algorithms work. Although social media platforms absolutely compound this feeling through their lack of transparency, Kyle makes the excellent point that our anxiety isn't actually about the algorithm itself, but rather about what the algorithm represents. We feel concern over censorship, surveillance, shortened attention spans, deindividualization, and harmful polarization, but these are only the negative emergent effects of human-algorithm interaction. It's right to be worried about them, but I would argue that there are absolutely positive effects, too.

The new symbol for "dog" isn't a bellwether indicating our collapse as a society. It's just a cool example of humans adapting to our environment, as we have always done throughout history.

Beyond that, it's a testament to the fact that there *is* a Deaf community online with such power and connectivity that they can indeed drive language change. That community exists because the algorithm brought them together in a filter bubble.

Social media isn't monolithically good or bad. It's a mess, like any new technology. Language change has always been beyond our control and shaped by invisible factors. Your preferences don't really matter, because linguistic evolution reflects cultural moments more than the feelings of individual people. Since our cultural moment is defined by social media algorithms, it makes sense that language also reflects that.

Back when I chose the title of this book, "algospeak" had already been floating around as a term for the kind of algorithmic censorship avoidance I describe in chapter 1. In fact, that was what first drew me into researching the language of social media: I was fascinated by what I could and couldn't say online. The more I thought about and researched my own career, however, the more I began to understand that every aspect of our language is now being shaped by algorithms.

Yes, the word "unalive" is an easy-to-point-to example of algospeak, in the same way that the new ASL symbol for "dog" is an identifiable example of short-form video reshaping communication. But "skibidi" and "delulu" and "cottagecore" and the tighter ASL gestures were all also algospeak. They were uniquely shaped by trends, memes, and filter bubbles that are reflective of the online space and that have gone beyond the internet into the offline world. The underlying patterns are the same as they've always been—humans tenaciously coming up with new ways to express themselves—but it's all happening in this entirely new medium and with rapid speed.

. . . . . . . . .

Every time I post a video talking about contemporary slang, I inevitably get the same comment: "We're so cooked." Ironically, this is also a new slang phrase, meaning "we're screwed." Perhaps out of algorithmic anxiety, or perhaps out of old-school grammatical purism, there seems to be a general sense that our language is evolving in the wrong direction, even when that flies in the face of how it is used in the real world. To that end, I'd like to respond with a quotation from the fourteenth-century poet Geoffrey Chaucer:

> 3e knowe ek that in fourme of speche is chaunge
> With-inne a thousand 3eer and wordes tho
> That hadden pris now wonder nyce and straunge
> Us thenketh hem and 3et thei spake hem so
> And spedde as wel in loue as men now do.

Roughly translated, that means the following:

> You know that the form of speech will change
> Within a thousand years, and words
> That were once apt, we now regard as quaint and strange
> And yet they spoke them thus
> And succeeded as well in love as men do now.

Chaucer's quotation perfectly encapsulates why I don't think that "we're cooked." No matter how much the form of speech changes, we will continue succeeding in love the same as we always have—in other words, we will continue to be human. "Algospeak" isn't so much a story about algorithms as it is about how *humans* adapt to those algorithms. Unsurprisingly, we've proven ourselves to be as human as ever. We've always had memes and trends and attention-grabbing techniques. We've always evaded censorship. We've always made in-groups and out-groups.

The story of mankind has always been told through the tools we create. The Stone Age, Bronze Age, and Iron Age caused dramatic shifts in how we lived our daily lives and reshaped our social structures. The Agricultural and Industrial Revolutions were accompanied by significant cultural upheavals and mass urbanization. We've always molded ourselves around these ages and revolutions, but certain innate characteristics are always there. We come up with ingenious new ways to use our tools, for both good and bad. Then language reflexively evolves around these new tools, helping us discuss and frame our reality.

Algorithms are yet another tool, and algospeak is a reflection of how we interact with that tool. We have all our new trendbait and SEO keywords and euphemisms because that is how we are currently harnessing that tool and retracing our old linguistic footsteps. We have incel language and Swiftie language and generational labels as emergent outgrowths of that tool, evolving as our natural behaviors mesh with it over time.

We are creative, damn it. Our language, culture, and identity are inevitably molded by our environment, but we work through those molds to keep doing silly, ingenious things with language, because we're resilient in our silliness and ingenuity. No matter what comes next, we'll continue to be the same: succeeding as well in love as we do now.

# ACKNOWLEDGMENTS

Whenever I sound too confident in my self-sufficiency, my mom always makes the same joke about how I must've popped out of the womb not needing any help because I already knew everything. To my parents, I won't make that mistake now: This book would not have happened without your excellent child-rearing abilities, unconditional support, and encouragement of knowledge seeking. Even if I don't call home enough, I deeply appreciate you.

To Kirkland, to the Beef, to my weird little friend groups: Keep being weird. It takes a weird environment for me to do what I do, from my earliest dolphin-click videos to my current research. Whether it's lurking incel forums or studying *Skibidi Toilet* or visiting middle school girls' clothing stores, I'm probably only still sane because I can share these moments with you all. Special shout-out to all the friends who have ever co-worked with me, because I can't hold myself accountable unless someone is making sure I don't accidentally start playing *Flappy Bird* instead of writing. I think that's John Sanchez, Joanna Boyland,

Simon Levien, Charlotte Daniels, Hayley Grape, Rachel Auslander, Hannah Martinez, and Alefiyah Gandhi (who also doubles as my photographer and etiquette coach).

To my literary agent, Rachel Vogel—you made my first time writing a book feel seamless and fun. Thanks for your unwavering support throughout the entire process. Same to my editor, Quynh Do, whose extremely helpful feedback shaped my writing to be much better than it otherwise would've been. Thanks to Matthew Sciarappa, Rob Shapiro, Jessica Purcell, and everybody else at Knopf and DCL who made this a hundred times easier. Thanks also to my U.K. agent, Rachel Clements at Abner Stein; my U.K. editor, Shammah Banerjee at Ebury; and my jacket designer, Tyler Comrie.

There were a few important decision moments catalyzed by people who might not even have realized their impact. I'm not sure that I ever would've started my TikTok if not for a random dhall conversation with Ian Kimbell, or ever thought to write a book unless I had seen Catherine Yeo do it first.

Thanks to the internet linguistics community for creating a welcoming environment online: Roy Bualan, Griffin Bassett, Yuval Ben-Hayun, and everybody else on LingTok. Thanks to Gretchen McCulloch, author of *Because Internet,* and Amanda Montell, author of *Wordslut,* for inspiring me through your books first. Thanks to my followers for bearing through my shaky fast-paced videos, and thanks to all the people who somehow agreed to be interviewed for this book.

Finally, to my readers. Keep being human and using language in new and exciting ways. Love you all.

# NOTES

### Introduction: Why Your Kids Are Saying "Unalive"

1. Jeff McMillan, "Online, 'Unalive' Means Death or Suicide. Experts Say It Might Help Kids Discuss Those Things," AP News, July 14, 2023.
2. "Unalive," Know Your Meme, knowyourmeme.com. Accessed December 22, 2024.
3. Sapna Maheshwaro, "Topics Suppressed in China Are Underrepresented on TikTok, Study Says," *New York Times,* Dec. 21, 2023; Alex Hern, "Revealed: How TikTok Censors Videos That Do Not Please Beijing," *Guardian,* Sept. 24, 2019.
4. Amelia Tait, "Are TikTok Algorithms Changing How People Talk About Suicide?," *Wired,* May 27, 2022.

### 1. How to Play Linguistic Whac-A-Mole

1. Sam Biddle et al., "Invisible Censorship: TikTok Told Moderators to Suppress Posts by 'Ugly' People and the Poor to Attract New Users," *Intercept,* March 16, 2020.
2. M+H Advisor, "Do Museums Deserve More Freedom on Social Media?," Museums and Heritage, March 31, 2022, museumsandheritage.com.
3. TikTok, "For You Feed Eligibility Standards," Community Guidelines, www.tiktok.com. Accessed December 22, 2024.
4. Emily van der Nagel, "'Networks That Work Too Well': Intervening in Algorithmic Connections," *Media International Australia* 168, no. 1 (2018): 81–92, doi.org/10.1177/1329878X18783002.
5. Priyanka Shanker et al., "Are Social Media Giants Censoring Pro-Palestine Voices amid Israel's War?," *Al Jazeera,* Oct. 24, 2023.

6.  Sam Shead, "TikTok Apologizes After Being Accused of Censoring #BlackLives Matter Posts," CNBC, June 2, 2020, www.cnbc.com.
7.  Chris Fox, "TikTok Admits Restricting Some LGBT Hashtags," BBC, Sept. 10, 2020.

## 2. Sticking Out Your Gyat for the Rizzler

1.  Laura Herman, "For Who Page? TikTok Creators' Algorithmic Dependencies," *IASDR 2023,* Oct. 2023, doi.org/10.21606/iasdr.2023.576.
2.  Ian Stewart and Jacob Eisenstein, "Making 'Fetch' Happen: The Influence of Social and Linguistic Context on Nonstandard Word Growth and Decline," *Proceedings of the 2018 Conference on Empirical Methods in Natural Language Processing, Brussels, Belgium* (Stroudsburg, Pa.: Association for Computational Linguistics, 2018), 4360–70, doi.org/10.18653/v1/D18-1467.
3.  Everett Rogers, *Diffusion of Innovations* (New York: Free Press of Glencoe, 1962).
4.  Allan Metcalf, *Predicting New Words: The Secrets of Their Success* (Boston: Houghton Mifflin, 2004).

## 3. No Because What Happened to Your Attention?

1.  Alex Moehring, "Personalization, Engagement, and Content Quality on Social Media: An Evaluation of Reddit's News Feed," OSF Preprints, May 30, 2024, doi.org/10.31219/osf.io/8yuwe.
2.  Jonah Berger and Katherine Milkman, "Social Transmission, Emotion, and the Virality of Online Content," Marketing Science Institute Working Paper Series 2010, Report No. 10-114, 2010, thearf-org-unified-admin.s3.amazonaws.com/MSI/2020/06/MSI_Report_10-114.pdf.
3.  William Brady et al., "Attentional Capture Helps Explain Why Moral and Emotional Content Go Viral," *Journal of Experimental Psychology* 149, no. 4 (April 2020), pubmed.ncbi.nlm.nih.gov/31486666/.
4.  Grant Packard and Jonah Berger, "Thinking of You: How Second-Person Pronouns Shape Cultural Success," *Psychological Science* 31, no. 4 (2020): 397–407, doi.org/10.1177/0956797620902380.
5.  Chantal Carpenter, "New Economics for Sustainable Development: Attention Economy," United Nations Economist Network, March 23, 2023.
6.  Arvind Narayanan, "Understanding Social Media Recommendation Algorithms," Knight First Amendment Institute at Columbia University, March 9, 2023, knightcolumbia.org.

## 4. Why Everybody Sounds the Same Online

1.  Jamie Doward, "Why You Shouldn't Get Salty if Your Child 'Speaks YouTube,'" *Guardian,* Sept. 13, 2020.
2.  Emily Matchar, "Finding What's 'Oddly Satisfying' on the Internet," *New York Times,* Feb. 22, 2019.
3.  Kate Lindsay, "Are You Sure You're Not Guilty of the 'Millennial Pause'?," *Atlantic,* Aug. 6, 2022.
4.  Jimmy Donaldson, "How to Succeed in MrBeast Production," drive.google.com/file/d/1YaG9xpu-WQKBPUi8yQ4HaDYQLUSa7Y3J/view. Accessed October 15, 2024.

5.   Sophia Smith Galer, "How TikTok Created a New Accent—and Why It Might Be the Future of English," BBC, Jan. 23, 2024.

6.   Julie Beck, "The Linguistics of 'YouTube Voice,'" *Atlantic,* Dec. 7, 2015.

## 5. "The Algorithm Really Knows Me"

1.   Pia Ceres, "Quoting Taylor Swift Lyrics Is an Actual Linguistic Thing," *Wired,* Feb. 3, 2023.

2.   Narayanan, "Understanding Social Media Recommendation Algorithms."

3.   Alice Marwick and Danah Boyd, "I Tweet Honestly, I Tweet Passionately: Twitter Users, Context Collapse, and the Imagined Audience," *New Media & Society* 13, no. 1 (2011), 114–33, doi.org/10.1177/1461444810365313.

4.   Sydney Lambert, "The TikTok Effect: How the Social Media App Helps Spread Autism Misinformation," National Council on Severe Autism, Oct. 18, 2023, www.ncsautism.org.

5.   Jonathan Stray et al., "The Algorithmic Management of Polarization and Violence on Social Media," Knight First Amendment Institute at Columbia University, Aug. 22, 2023, knightcolumbia.org.

6.   Jeremy Frimer et al., "Incivility Is Rising Among American Politicians on Twitter," *Social Psychological and Personality Science* 14, no. 2 (2023): 259–69, doi.org/10.1177/19485506221083811.

## 6. Wordpilled Slangmaxxing

1.   Michael Halpin, "Weaponized Subordination: How Incels Discredit Themselves to Degrade Women," *Gender & Society* 36, no. 6 (2022): 813–37, doi.org/10.1177/0891243222112854.

2.   "Rape," Incels Wiki, incels.wiki/w/Rape. Accessed October 21, 2024.

3.   "R9k," Incels Wiki, incels.wiki/w/R9k. Accessed October 21, 2024.

4.   Steffi Cao, "Trolls Are Citing an 'Oxford Study' to Demean Asian Women in Interracial Relationships. But It Doesn't Actually Exist," *Guardian,* June 12, 2024.

5.   Aidan Walker, "Where Do Memes Come From? The Top Platforms from 2010–2022," KnowYourMeme, 2022.

6.   Emerging Technology from the arXiv, "This Is Where Internet Memes Come From," *MIT Technology Review,* June 11, 2018.

7.   "Discussion: Imagine if the Internet Was Never Invented," Involuntary Celibate Forum, June 21, 2024, incels.is.

## 7. It's Giving Appropriation

1.   Robert Thompson, "An Aesthetic of the Cool," *African Arts* 7, no. 1 (Aug. 1973), www.jstor.org/stable/3334749?origin=JSTOR-pdf.

2.   José Criales-Unzueta, "From Underground Subculture to Global Phenomenon: An Oral History of Ballroom Within Mainstream Culture," *Vogue,* June 28, 2023.

3.   Teresa Correa and Sun Ho Jeong, "Race and Online Content Creation," *Information, Communication & Society* 14, no. 5 (2011): 638–59, doi.org/10.1080/1369118X.2010.514355.

4.   "Hood Irony," Know Your Meme, knowyourmeme.com/memes/hood-irony. Accessed December 22, 2024.

5.  John Blake, "What's 'Digital Blackface'? And Why Is It Wrong When White People Use It?," CNN, March 26, 2023, www.cnn.com.
6.  "What Is Blaccent and Why Do People Keep Using It?," *PBS Origins*, PBS, April 11, 2022, www.pbs.org.
7.  Michael Arceneaux, "On the Exploitation of Black Genius: It's Time for Peaches 'On Fleek' Monroee to Collect Her Check," *Essence*, Oct. 26, 2020.

### 8. What Are We Wearing This Summer?

1.  "Core Suffix," Aesthetics Wiki, aesthetics.fandom.com/wiki/Category:Core _Suffix. Accessed October 21, 2024.
2.  "Subcultures Are the New Demographics," *TikTok for Business* (blog), July 29, 2021, ads.tiktok.com.
3.  Chris Anderson, "The Long Tail," *Wired*, Oct. 1, 2004.
4.  Medline Shulz, "Did Micro-trends Kill the Trend Cycle?," *Vogue Business*, June 12, 2024.
5.  Rebecca Jennings, "Against Trendbait," *Vox*, Feb. 7, 2024.
6.  Callie Holtermann, "Why Do We Brand the Summer?," *New York Times*, June 3, 2023.
7.  Caroline Bourque, "The Making of a Microtrend," *Business of Home*, Aug. 2, 2023, businessofhome.com.
8.  Cory Doctorow, "The 'Enshittification' of TikTok," *Wired*, Jan. 23, 2023.
9.  Cory Doctorow, "'Enshittification' Is Coming for Absolutely Everything," *FT Magazine*, Feb. 8, 2024.
10. "Algorithmic Attention Rents," UCL Institute for Innovation and Public Purpose, www.ucl.ac.uk. Accessed August 26, 2024.
11. Kendall Walton, "Categories of Art," *Philosophical Review* 79, no. 3 (1970): 334–67, www.jstor.org/stable/2183933.

### 9. OK Boomer

1.  Samantha Raphelson, "From GIs to Gen Z (or Is It iGen?): How Generations Get Nicknames," NPR, Oct. 6, 2014, www.npr.org.
2.  Joe Pinsker, "'Gen Z' Only Exists in Your Head," *Atlantic*, Oct. 14, 2021.
3.  Madison Malone Kircher, "Gen Alpha Is Here. Can You Understand Their Slang?," *New York Times*, Nov. 8, 2023.
4.  William Brady et al., "Social-Media Algorithms Have Hijacked 'Social Learning,'" Kellogg School of Management, Aug. 16, 2023, insight.kellogg.northwestern .edu.
5.  Eleanor Cummins, "The Creepy TikTok Algorithm Doesn't Know You," *Wired*, Jan. 3, 2022.

### 10. Are We Cooked?

1.  Elian Peltier, "How Africans Are Changing French—One Joke, Rap, and Book at a Time," *New York Times*, Dec. 12, 2023.
2.  Stephen McDonell, "Why China Censors Banned Winnie the Pooh," BBC, July 17, 2017, www.bbc.com.
3.  Chaya Hiruncharoenvate et al., "Algorithmically Bypassing Censorship on Sina Weibo with Nondeterministic Homophone Substitutions," *Proceedings of the*

*International AAAI Conference on Web and Social Media* 9, no. 1 (2015): 150–58, doi.org/10.1609/icwsm.v9i1.14637.

4. Rodney Jones and Dennis Chau, "Metalinguistic Tactics in the Hong Kong Protest Movement," *Journal of Language and Politics* 21, no. 1 (2022): 143–72, doi .org/10.1075/jlp.21017.jon.

5. John Wilford, "Languages Die, but Not Their Last Words," *New York Times,* Sept. 19, 2007.

6. Chitra Ramaswamy, "Regional Dialects Are Dying Out—It's Enough to Get You Blarting," *Guardian,* May 30, 2016.

7. Lars Hinrichs et al., "Real-Time Trends in the Texas English Vowel System: F2 Trajectory in GOOSE as an Index of a Variety's Ongoing Delocalization," *Rice Working Papers in Linguistics* 4 (Fall 2013), wellformedness.com/papers/hinrichs -etal-2013.pdf.

8. Amanda Morris, "How a Visual Language Evolves as Our World Does," *New York Times,* July 26, 2022.

9. Amanda Morris, "Fake Sign Language Is Spreading on TikTok. Deaf People Are Worried," *Washington Post,* May 8, 2023.

# Index

Page numbers in *italics* refer to charts and illustrations.

## A Note About the Author

ADAM ALEKSIC is a linguist and content creator posting educational videos as the "Etymology Nerd" to an audience of more than two million. As a linguistics student at Harvard College, he founded and served as president of the Harvard Undergraduate Linguistics Society. He's discussed online language on NPR and repeatedly contributed to *The Washington Post,* and his work has been mentioned in *The New York Times, The Economist,* and *The Guardian.* He's lectured on language and social media at Stanford, Yale, Georgetown, and other top universities, including a TEDx talk at the University of Pennsylvania. Aleksic is based in New York City, where he spends a lot of time scrolling TikTok for "research."

## A Note on the Type

This book was set in Minion, a typeface produced by the Adobe Corporation specifically for the Macintosh personal computer and released in 1990. Designed by Robert Slimbach, Minion combines the classic characteristics of old-style faces with the full complement of weights required for modern typesetting.

Composed by North Market Street Graphics
Lancaster, Pennsylvania

Designed by Marisa Nakasone